1153   18-

Index to
Fairfax County, Virginia
Wills and Fiduciary Records
1742 -1855

compiled by

Constance Ring
Archivist
Fairfax County Circuit Court

Willow Bend Bo
Lovettsville, Virg
1995

D1210999

Copyright © 1995. All rights reserved.
Willow Bend Books
39475 Tollhouse Road
Route 1, Box 15A
Lovettsville, Virginia 22080-9703

Printed in the United States of America

ISBN Number: 1-888265-02-7
Library of Congress Catalog Card Number: 95-62146

INTRODUCTION

This publication consists of an alphabetical index to wills and probate records of the Fairfax County Court during the period 1742 to 1855 and the Superior Court during the period 1809 to 1855. The wills and other probate records referred to in this volume are contained in bound will books, with some exceptions; loose papers identified by an asterisk "*" in the listing, administration bonds contained in a bound volume covering the period 1752 to 1782, chancery files (CFF#), deed books, Land Records of Long Standing (LRLS) and Proceedings in Land Causes (PLC). These records are all housed in the Fairfax Circuit Court Archives.

Information pertaining to a particular entry may be obtained by writing Archives, Circuit Court, 4110 Chain Bridge Road, Fairfax, VA 22030. Copies are available for a fee.

Microfilm copies of the referenced records may be found in the Virginia Room, Fairfax City Regional Library, Fairfax, Va. and the Library of Virginia, Richmond, Va. Microfilm is available through interlibrary loan from the Library of Virginia. A fee may be required. Reel numbers are identified in the following list of will and land records. Microfilm is also available through the LDS Family History Centers. Researchers should consult the Family History Library Catalog for film numbers at one of these centers.

Abbreviations

*	copy of document is located in Drawer X, Fairfax Circuit Court Archives
acct.	account
admr.	administrator
adv.	adversus (refers to defendant)
Bond Bk.	Bond Book, 1752-1782
CFF#	Chancery Final File number
Co.	county
C.O.B	Court Order Book (or Minute Book)
div.	division
est. acct.	estate account
exor.	executor
dau.	daughter
FDB	Fairfax Deed Book
Fx.	Fairfax
gdn.	guardian
LRLS	Land Records of Long Standing
PLC	Proceedings in Land Causes
Sup. Ct.	Superior Court Will Book, 1809-64
WB	Will Book

All county references are for Virginia unless otherwise noted.

Chronology of Will and Land Records

WILL BOOKS

Will Book, A1, Part 1	1742-1752	reel 27
Will Book, A1, Part 2	1742-1752	
Will Book, B1	1752-1767	
Will Book, C1	1767-1776	
Will Book, D1	1776-1782	reel 28
Will Book, E1	1783-1791	
Will Book, F1	1791-1794	
Will Book, G1	1794-1799	reel 29
Will Book, H1	1799-1801	
Will Book, J1	1801-1806	reel 30
Will Book, K1	1806-1812	
Will Book, L1	1816-1820	
Will Book, M1	1822-1825	
Will Book, N1	1825-1827	reel 31
Will Book, O1	1827-1830	
Will Book, Q1	1830-1832	reel 32
Will Book, R1	1832-1836	
Will Book, S1	1836-1838	reel 33
Will Book, T1	1839-1842	
Will Book, U1	1842-1846	
Will Book, V1	1846-1850	reel 34
Will Book, W1	1850-1853	
Will Book, X1	1853-1855	
Will Book, Y1	1855-1858	
Will Book, Z1	1858-1866	reel 35

Superior Court Will Book, 1809-64 (reel 35)

Bond Book, 1752-82 (reel 47).

LAND RECORDS

Deed Book, Liber A1, Part 1	1742-1746	reel 1
Deed Book, Liber A1, Part 2	1742-1746	
Deed Book, Liber B1	1746-1750	
Deed Book, Liber C1	1750-1754	reel 2
Deed Book, Liber D1	1755-1761	reel 3
Deed Book, Liber E1	1761-1763	
Deed Book, Liber F1	missing	
Deed Book, Liber G1	1765-1768	
Deed Book, Liber H1	missing	
Deed Book, Liber I1	missing	
Deed Book, Liber J1	missing	
Deed Book, Liber K1	1772-1773	reel 4
Deed Book, Liber L1	1773-1774	
Deed Book, Liber M1	1774-1777	
Deed Book, Liber N1	missing	
Deed Book, Liber O1	1783-1784	
Deed Book, Liber P1	1784-1785	reel 5
Deed Book, Liber Q1	1785-1788	
Deed Book, Liber R1	1788-1789	
Deed Book, Liber S1	1789-1790	reel 6
Deed Book, Liber T1	1790-1792	
Deed Book, Liber U1	1792-1793	
Deed Book, Liber V1	not used	
Deed Book, Liber W1	1793-1794	reel 7
Deed Book, Liber X1	1794-1795	
Deed Book, Liber Y1	1795-1796	reel 8
Deed Book, Liber Z1	1796-1797	
Deed Book, Liber A2	1797-1798	reel 9
Deed Book, Liber B2	1798-1800	
Deed Book, Liber C2	missing	
Deed Book, Liber D2	missing	

Deed Book, Liber E2	1803-1805	
Deed Book, Liber F2	missing	
Deed Book, Liber G2	1806-1807	reel 10
Deed Book, Liber H2	missing	
Deed Book, Liber I2	missing	
Deed Book, Liber J2	1808-1810	
Deed Book, Liber K2	missing	
Deed Book, Liber L2	1811-1812	
Deed Book, Liber M2	1812-1813	reel 11
Deed Book, Liber N2	missing	
Deed Book, Liber 02	1815-1817	
Deed Book, Liber P2	1817-1818	
Deed Book, Liber Q2	missing	
Deed Book, Liber R2	1819-1820	
Deed Book, Liber S2	1820-1821	reel 12
Deed Book, Liber T2	1821-1822	
Deed Book, Liber U2	1822-1823	
Deed Book, Liber V2	1824-1825	
Deed Book, Liber W2	1825-1826	reel 13
Deed Book, Liber X2	1826-1828	
Deed Book, Liber Y2	1828-1830	reel 14
Deed Book, Liber Z2	1830-1831	
Deed Book, Liber A3	1831-1833	reel 15
Deed Book, Liber B3	1833-1835	
Deed Book, Liber C3	1835-1836	reel 16
Deed Book, Liber D3	1836-1838	
Deed Book, Liber E3	1838-1839	reel 17
Deed Book, Liber F3	1839-1841	
Deed Book, Liber G3	1841-1842	
Deed Book, Liber H3	1842-1844	reel 18
Deed Book, Liber I3	1844	

LAND RECORDS (continued)

Deed Book, Liber J3	1844-1845	
Deed Book, Liber K3	1845-1846	reel 19
Deed Book, Liber L3	1846-1847	
Deed Book, Liber M3	1847-1848	
Deed Book, Liber N3	1848-1849	
Deed Book, Liber 03	1849-1850	
Deed Book, Liber P3	1851-1852	
Deed Book, Liber Q3	1851-1852	reel 20
Deed Book, Liber R3	1852-1853	reel 21
Deed Book, Liber S3	1853	
Deed Book, Liber T3	1853-1854	
Deed Book, Liber U3	1854	reel 22
Deed Book, Liber V3	1854-1855	
Deed Book, Liber W3	1855	
Deed Book, Liber X3	1855-1856	reel 23
Deed Book, Liber Y3	1856-1857	
Deed Book, Liber Z3	1857-1858	
Deed Book, Liber A4	1858-1859	reel 24
Deed Book, Liber B4	1859-1860	
Deed Book, Liber C4	1860-1861	
Deed Book, Liber D4	1861-1862	reel 25

[pages 1 to 181 cover 1861 to 1862;
pages 195-454 cover 1788 to 1822]

| Deed Book, Liber E4 | 1863-1865 | |

Land Records of Long Standing, 1742-70   reel 46

Land Causes No. 1, 1788-1824, 1812-32   reel 46

Note: Reel numbers refer to Libary of Virginia roll numbers

Name	Document	Will Book	Page
ABERCROMBIE			
Robert	will	N	202
ADAM			
James	est. acct.	E	211
	inventory	F	147
Jane	gdn. bond	F	88
	gdn. acct.	F	307
	gdn. acct.	G	64, 143
John	gdn. bond	F	88
	gdn. acct.	F	307
	gdn. acct.	G	641, 143
Robert	will	E	315
	exor. bond	E	318
	legatees gdn. acct.	F	307
	admr. acct.	F	330
	legatees gdn. acct.	G	64, 143
	est. acct.	I	147
Robert	gdn. bond	F	88
	gdn. acct.	F	307
	gdn. acct.	G	64, 143
ADAMS			
Abednego	will	I	228
	est. acct.	K	148
Ann	will	P	11
	inventory	P	141
	est. acct.	P	377
Eleanor	will	A1 pt. 2	346
	admr. bond	A1 pt. 2	347
	inventory	A1 pt. 2	380
Francis	will	K	62
Francis Jr.	gdn. bond	I	311
Francis P.	gdn. bond	L	119
(son of George)	gdn. bond	O	49
Francis T.	gdn. bond	I	417

Name	Document	Will Book	Page
ADAMS (continued)			
Gabriel	exor. bond	A1 pt. 2	427
	will	A1 pt. 2	428
	inventory	A1 pt. 2	446
	est. acct.	B	81
Gabriel	will	U	242
	sale acct.	U	252*
	inventory	U	254
	est. acct.	V	286
	est. acct.	W	368*
George	est. acct.	O	217
George	gdn. bond	O	49
(son of George)	gdn. bond	Q	203
Hannah	will	N	81
	inventory	N	367
John	inventory	A1 pt. 2	497
	est. acct.	B	69
John	gdn. bond	F	88
John	inventory	V	368
	sale acct.	V	369
	est. acct.	W	324*
Louisa	gdn. bond	O	49
(dau. of George)	gdn. bond	Q	203
Mary Ann	will	M	403
Samuel	will	I	416
	inventory	J	28
	est. acct.	J	298
Samuel	will	T	202
	est. acct.	U	67
	distrib. acct.	U	68
	inventory	U	279
	sale acct.	U	281
Sarah L.	gdn. bond	L	119
(dau. of George)	gdn. bond	O	49
William	will	Sup. Ct.	5
	exor. bond	Sup. Ct.	8
	inventory	Sup. Ct.	12

Name	Document	Will Book	Page
ADAMS (continued)			
William	sale acct.	Sup. Ct.	15
	est. acct.	Sup. Ct.	19
William G.	gdn. bond	I	311
AGER			
Ann	renunciation of husband		
	Samuel's will	M	84
John	gdn. bond	R	153
John L.	gdn. acct.	T	269
Samuel	will	M	70
	inventory	M	215
	admr. bond	M	251
	est. acct.	M	290
	est. acct. (corrected - see CFF#1y -		
	Ager vs. Hopkins - 1836)		
Sarah F.	gdn. bond	R	153
AINSWORTH			
George	admr. bond	G	307
ALEXANDER			
Austin	gdn. bond	F	126
Garrard	will	B	327
Garrard	gdn. bond	F	126
George Dent	will	E	150
George Dent	gdn. bond	F	126
John	will (partial)		
	(see FDB P1:397)		
John S.	will	H	138
	inventory	H	178
Lucinda W.	gdn. bond	J	193
Mary	will	F	222
Philip	will	E	373
	exor. bond	E	374
	inventory	E	413
	sale acct.	F	19

Name	Document	Will Book	Page
ALEXANDER (continued)			
Philip	gdn. bond	F	126
Robert	will (1736 - Stafford Co. - see LRLS:172)		
Robert	will (1793)	F	219
Walter	gdn. bond	H	132
Walter	est. acct.	J	421
William (of Effingham)	will (1813 - Prince William Co. - see FDB V2:19)		
ALLEN			
Andrew	will	J	327
	est. acct.	J	428
	inventory	L	49
James W.	sale acct.	X	50
	inventory	X	51
	est. acct.	X	52*
Thomas	will	W	253
	inventory	W	298
ALLISON			
Amanda	gdn. bond	R	133
	gdn. acct.	S	119
Andrew	gdn. bond	R	133
	gdn. acct.	S	119
	gdn. bond	V	293
George W.	gdn. bond	R	133
	gdn. acct.	S	119
	gdn. acct.	T	150
	gdn. acct.	U	12, 227
	gdn. acct.	V	152, 254
Harrison	will	Sup. Ct.	66
	admr. bond	Sup. Ct.	67
	inventory	Sup. Ct.	90
	sale acct.	Sup. Ct.	92
	est. acct.	Sup. Ct.	96, 106, 115, 116, 121

Name	Document	Will Book	Page
ALLISON (continued)			
Harrison	gdn. acct.	S	119
	est. acct.	U	14
James R.	gdn. bond	P	341
John	admr. bond	I	95
	inventory	K	42
	admr. acct.	K	43
John	div. of slaves	U	100
	inventory	U	206
	sale acct.	U	208
	est. acct.	U	318*
Martha	gdn. bond	V	292
Martha Ann	gdn. acct.	U	13
Porter	gdn. acct.	S	119, 307
Sinah Ann	gdn. bond	R	133
	gdn. acct.	S	119
	gdn. acct.	T	150
	gdn. acct.	U	227
	gdn. acct.	V	152, 254
Thomas	will	K	40
	exor. bond	K	49
	inventory	K	91
Thompson	will	R	330
William	will	K	39
	inventory	N	230
ALTON			
John	will	E	188
ANDERSON			
John	inventory	I	50
William	inventory	E	255
APPLETON			
John	inventory	A1 pt. 2	378
	est. acct.	A1 pt. 2	443
Mary	admr. bond	A1 pt. 2	318

Name	Document	Will Book	Page
ARBUTHNOT			
Thomas	will	A1 pt. 1	3
	exor. bond	A1 pt. 1	4
	inventory	A1 pt. 1	6
	est. acct.	A1 pt. 1	50, 242
ARDIS			
Joshua	admr. bond	Bond Bk.	133
ARELL			
Christiana	gdn. bond	G	137
David	will	F	79
	exor. bond	F	82
	inventory	F	262
Richard	gdn. bond	G	137
Richard	admr. bond	G	141
Samuel	will	G	130
	exor. bond	G	140
ARMS			
Aaron	admr. bond	G	53
ARUNDELL (or ARUNDLE)			
Jemima	inventory	V	341
	sale acct.	V	344
	est. acct.*		
John	will	M	372
	inventory	V	340
	sale acct.	V	347
Peter	gdn. bond	R	203
ASHFORD			
Elizabeth	admr. bond	Bond Bk.	124
	inventory	C	195
Francis	will	V	69
	inventory	V	289

Name	Document	Will Book	Page

ASHFORD (continued)
George	gdn. bond	A1 pt. 1	32
John	inventory	B	415
	est. acct.	B	417
	admr. bond	Bond Bk.	74
Michael	will	G	2

ASHTON
Henry	will (1730 - Westmoreland Co. - see PLC #2:55-61)		
John W.	will	S	212
	inventory	T	169
	est. acct. (see CFF#62r - Murray vs. Ashton - 1846)		

ASKEW
| John | admr. bond | Bond Bk. | 87 |

ASKINS
John	will	G	223
	exor. bond	G	224
	inventory	G	321

ATCHISON
Margaret	will	W	80
	inventory	W	87
Sarah	gdn. bond	M	50

ATHEY
James B.	inventory	K	66
William B.	inventory	U	197
	sale acct.	U	198
	est. acct.	V	247

AULD
| Colin | will | T | 210 |

Name	Document	Will Book	Page
AVERY			
Michael	gdn. bond	H	58
Philip	gdn. bond	H	58
Polly	gdn. bond	H	58
Samuel	gdn. bond	H	58
AWBREY			
George	will	B	51
John	will	A1 pt. 1	60
	exor. bond	A1 pt. 1	64
	est. acct.	A1 pt. 2	501
Richard	will	A1 pt. 1	79
	admr. bond	A1 pt. 1	81
	inventory	A1 pt. 1	104
BAGGETTT			
Ignatius	inventory	D	397
BAILEY see BAYLEY			
BAILISS see BAYLISS			
BAKER			
Giles	will	M	127
	inventory	M	218
Joshua	will	U	89
	inventory	U	99
BALL			
James T.	exor. bond	S	216
John	will	B	422
	inventory	B	437
	est. acct.	C	137
Moses	will	F	176
Mottrom	inventory	U	149
	sale acct.	U	151
	est. acct.	U	321
	div. of slaves	W	251

Name	Document	Will Book	Page
BALLENDINE			
John	will	D	247
	inventory	E	302, 303
	sale acct. (Falls)	E	304
	sale acct. (Etrick Bank)	E	307
	est. acct.	E	308
BALLENGER			
Daniel Mills	inventory	D	74
	est. acct.	D	93
	admr. bond	Bond Bk.	159b
Francis	inventory	U	250*
	sale acct. est. acct.*	U	251*
Judith	admr. bond	A1 pt. 1	166
	inventory	A1 pt. 1	177
	est. acct.	A1 pt. 1	252
William	will	D	92
	inventory	D	107
BALMAIN			
Andrew	inventory	J	348
BALSER			
Gasper	will	D	417
	inventory	D	425
BARDEN			
James	will	W	254
	div. of slaves	W	302
	est. acct.	X	199*
John	will	R	145
	inventory	R	151
	sale acct.	R	406
	est. acct.	S	151
	est. acct.	U	312*

Name	Document	Will Book	Page
BARKER			
Ann	inventory	L	61
	will	U	98
	inventory	U	129
	sale acct.	U	146
Anna	est. acct.	R	288
Barbara	will	Q	235
	inventory	Q	385
	sale acct.	Q	387
Eleanor	inventory	M	265
	est. acct.	N	2
John	admr. bond	F	185
	inventory	I	84
	sale acct.	I	87
	est. acct.	I	89
John B.	will	I	437
	inventory	J	119
	inventory	K	211
	sale acct.	L	359
Leonard	inventory	Q	339
	sale acct.	Q	342
	est. acct.	R	173
Matilda	gdn. bond	P	256
Moses	will	F	199
	exor. bond	F	200
	est. acct.	G	21
	inventory	G	22
Nathaniel	will	H	229
	admr. bond	H	230
	inventory	I	153
Nathaniel	will	R	93
	inventory	R	134
	est. acct.	S	116
	distribution acct.	S	118
	sale acct. (see CFF#30u - Follin's admrs. vs. Barker's exr. - 1842)		

Name	Document	Will Book	Page
BARKER (continued)			
Unice	inventory	M	272
	est. acct.	N	1
William	will	H	83
	est. acct.	H	207
	inventory	H	210
	sale acct.	H	213
William	will	L	374
	inventory	L	393
	est. acct.	M	266
BARNES			
Abraham	will	E	73
	inventory	E	85
Casandra	est. acct.	R	51
	est. acct.	U	310*
	est. acct.	V	208
John	inventory	N	333
	sale acct.	N	336
	est. acct.	O	251
	est. acct.	Q	35
John	inventory	U	330*
Sarah	will	E	158
	inventory	E	171
BARNET			
Thomas	will	B	96
BARRETT			
Edward	admr. bond	Bond Bk.	83
BARRICK			
Lewis	inventory	L	287
	sale acct.	L	288
	est. acct.	L	290

Name	Document	Will Book	Page
BARRY			
Edward	will	A1 pt. 1	227
	admr. bond	A1 pt. 1	237
	inventory	A1 pt. 1	249
	div. & settlement (see FDB C:774)		
John	inventory	C	246
	div. of est.	D	79
	admr. bond	Bond Bk.	146
Sarah	gdn. bond	E	21
BATES			
Edward	will	B	332
	inventory	B	335
Edward	will	K	90
	inventory	K	257
	sale acct.	L	346
	est. acct.	L	349
Jane	inventory	U	371
John	inventory	D	137
	admr. bond	Bond Bk.	168
Milly	gdn. bond	E	164
Thomas	will	S	227
	inventory	S	486
	sale acct.	U	373
BAYLEY			
Robert	inventory	D	269
	admr. bond	Bond Bk.	181
Samuel	sale acct.	L	220
	est. acct.	M	271
William	will	D	439
	inventory	E	167
BAYLISS			
Mildred	inventory	U	115
	sale acct.	U	118
	admr. bond	Sup. Ct.	127

Name	Document	Will Book	Page
BAYLISS (continued)			
Thomas	will	D	155
	inventory	D	172
	est. acct.	I	141
	inventory	J	102
William P.	inventory	J	108
BEACH			
Charles	inventory	J	418
	sale acct.	J	419
Charles	inventory	P	280
	sale acct.	P	281
	est. acct.	Q	373
Charles W.	est. acct.	M	255
James	admr. bond	A1 pt. 1	38
	inventory	A1 pt. 1	41
	est. acct.	A1 pt. 1	70
John	inventory	X	185
Lewis	will	X	30*
Solomon	inventory	P	20
	est. acct.	P	332
	sale acct.	P	413
Thomas	will	E	406
	exor. bond	E	408
	inventory	E	411
William	inventory	U	113
	sale acct.	U	114
BEALL			
Sophia	will	D	326
	inventory	D	338
Upton	will	O	427
BEARD			
George	gdn. bond	J	393
	gdn. bond	O	411

Name	Document	Will Book	Page
BEARD (continued)			
George	inventory	K	280
	inventory	L	15
	sale acct.	L	19
	est. acct.	L	34
	sale acct.	M	316
	est. acct.	M	319
George	will	U	183
Sarah	gdn. bond	J	393
William	gdn. bond	J	393
BECK			
Susan(nah)	will	P	421
	inventory	Q	99
	sale acct.	Q	102
	est. acct.	Q	329
BECKWITH			
Jennings	gdn. bond	H	126
Marmaduke	inventory	I	41
	sale acct.	L	314
	est. acct.	L	335
	est. acct.	M	340
	est. acct.	P	51, 291
	est. acct.	T	22, 24, 25
Newman	admr. bond	Sup. Ct.	119
Sybil	inventory	O	167
	sale acct.	P	16
	est. acct.	P	54, 294
Tapley	gdn. bond	H	152
William	gdn. bond	H	125
BEECH see **BEACH**			
BEELER			
Christopher	will	D	129

Name	Document	Will Book	Page
BELL			
William	will	J	418
BELT			
William S.	inventory	P	208
	sale acct.	P	214
	est. acct.	P	315
BENNETT			
Charles	will (1762 - Dumfries District Court - see FDB W1:74)		
Charles	will	T	72*
Dozier	inventory	P	90
	est. acct.	P	165
Elizabeth	will	E	188
	inventory	E	211
Joseph	will	F	287
	admr. bond	F	288
Joseph	inventory	S	389
Thomas	admr. bond	A1 pt. 1	2
	inventory	A1 pt. 1	5
	est. acct.	A1 pt. 1	6
BERKLEY			
Barbary	will (1785 - Loudoun Co.)*		
Barbary	gdn. bond	N	205
Benjamin	will	L	278*
	inventory	L	312
	est. acct.	N	288
Burgess	inventory	B	90
	admr. bond	Bond Bk.	23
Catharine	gdn. bond	P	257
Edriss	gdn. bond	M	30
George N.	will	Q	85
	inventory	Q	395
	sale acct.	Q	402
	est. acct.	R	120
	list of debts due	R	362

Name	Document	Will Book	Page
BERKLEY (continued)			
John	will	J	175
	inventory	J	264
	div. of est.	J	270, 432
	est. acct.	J	431
Julia	will*		
William	will	B	309
	inventory	B	331
	est. acct.	C	125
BERRY			
Tholomiah	est. acct.	Q	46
BERRYMAN			
Benjamin	will	A1 pt. 1	258
	exor. bond	A1 pt. 1	259
	inventory	A1 pt. 2	274
BETHEN			
David	admr. bond	A1 pt. 1	158
	inventory	A1 pt. 1	185
BEVIS			
Zachariah	admr. bond	A1 pt. 2	352
	inventory	A1 pt. 2	390
BIXLER			
John	will	T	379
	inventory	U	29
BLACK			
Alexander	admr. bond	Bond Bk.	141
Thomas	admr. bond	F	36
BLACKBURN			
Edward	est. acct.	I	488
	inventory	I	496

Name	Document	Will Book	Page
BLACKBURN (continued)			
Edward Lewis	will	P	7
	inventory (Fairfax Co.)	P	283
	inventory (Hampshire Co.)	P	286
	sale acct.	P	285, 289
	est. acct.	Q	77, 80
	est. acct.	S	291
	est. acct.	T	162
James L.	gdn. bond	S	468
Lee Ann	gdn. bond	S	468
	gdn. bond	W	253
Margaret	admr. bond	Bond Bk.	156
Mary Elizabeth	gdn. bond	S	468
Thomas	inventory	K	163
	est. acct.	L	71, 73
BLATT			
John	will	D	415
	inventory	E	84
BLINCOE			
Catharine Frances	gdn. bond	O	377
George Henry	gdn. bond	O	377
George W.	inventory	P	192
	sale acct.	P	192
Sybil	gdn. bond	O	377
William T.	gdn. bond	O	377
BLOSS			
Adam	will	F	76
	exor. bond	F	78
	inventory	I	477
	sale acct.	I	480
	est. acct.	I	484, 486

Name	Document	Will Book	Page
BLOXHAM			
James	admr. bond	F	203
	inventory	F	238
William	will	X	25
BLUNDLE see BLUNDON			
BLUNDON			
Elisha	inventory	J	121
Elisha	gdn. bond	O	393
John	est. acct.	R	161
William	gdn. bond	O	393
Winnifred	gdn. bond	O	393
BLYSTONE			
William	gdn. bond	E	243
BODKIN			
Washington Lee	gdn. bond	Q	277
William	will	P	261
BOGGESS			
Henry	inventory	E	118
Robert	inventory	C	154
	sale acct.	C	218
	est. acct.	C	219
	admr. bond	Bond Bk.	118
Robert	gdn. bond	E	65
Robert	will	F	140
Robert	will	L	142*
	inventory	L	153
	est. acct.	P	229
Sarah	will	J	32
	inventory	J	335
	est. acct.	L	399

Name	Document	Will Book	Page
BOLING			
Elizabeth	admr. bond	Bond Bk.	40
Robert	will	A1 pt. 1	185
	admr. bond	A1 pt. 1	186
	inventory	A1 pt. 1	189, 194
BOLLING			
Gerrard	will	D	159
	inventory	D	221
	admr. bond	Bond Bk.	176
Gerrard Jr.	inventory	D	221
John	inventory	D	143
	admr. bond	Bond Bk.	164
Joseph	inventory	B	128
	sale acct.	B	129
	est. acct.	B	193
	admr. bond	Bond Bk.	7
Miriam	dowry in slaves	H	240
Samuel	gdn. bond	E	121
Samuel	will	H	137
	inventory	H	239
	sale acct.	I	91
	est. acct.	J	220
	div. of est.	J	349
Simon	will	E	129
William	admr. bond	Bond Bk.	28
BOND			
Thomas	will	F	323
BONTZ			
Jacob	inventory	J	388
	sale acct.	J	435

BOSMAN see BOZMAN

Name	Document	Will Book	Page
BOSWELL			
Ann	inventory	J	94
Matthew	will	O	166
	inventory	O	210
	sale acct.	O	212
	est. acct.	P	169
BOUCHER			
Alexander	inventory	R	157
	est. acct.	R	255
BOWLING see **BOLING, BOLLING**			
BOWMAKER			
James	will	C	102
	inventory	C	107
BOZMAN			
Mary	will	B	57
	inventory	B	63
Thomas	will	B	55
	inventory	B	61
BRADLEY			
Ann Matilda	gdn. bond	T	230
	gdn. acct.	U	175
Catharine	gdn. bond	S	92
James	will	M	196
Jane M.	gdn. bond	Q	107
Peter B.	inventory	S	484
	sale acct.	T	271
William	inventory	D	6
	admr. bond	Bond Bk.	145
BRADT			
Susan C.	gdn. acct.	U	424

Name	Document	Will Book	Page
BRAWNER			
Mary	will	B	399
	inventory	B	404
	est. acct.	B	406
Thomas	inventory	K	173
	sale acct.	K	173
	est. acct.	K	189
BREWER			
Elizabeth	gdn. bond	L	59
John	gdn. bond	L	59
John	will	L	136*
	inventory	L	162
William	inventory	P	273
	sale acct.	P	275
	est. acct.	P	314
William	will	X	405
BREWSTER			
Mary	will	I	396
	inventory	I	411
Thomas	see BRUSTON, Thomas		
BREWSTER see also **BRUESTER**			
BRIGHT			
Wendall	will	E	38
	inventory	E	82
BRIM			
John	will	N	33*
	inventory	N	330
	sale acct.	N	332
BRITTON			
George	will	L	242
	inventory	L	339

Name	Document	Will Book	Page
BRITTON (continued)			
George (cont'd)	sale acct.	L	340
	est. acct.	L	351
	est. acct.	P	381
Fanny	gdn. bond	L	245
Hannah	gdn. bond	L	245
Keziah	accepts provisions of husband		
	George's will	L	277
Patty	gdn. bond	L	245
Samuel	gdn. bond	L	245
BROADWATER			
Ann C.	gdn. bond	Q	21
Arthur	gdn. bond	R	146
	gdn. acct.	S	171
	gdn. bond	S	457
Charles	will	I	471
	inventory	L	84*
	sale acct.	L	87
	est. acct.	L	112*
Charles G.	sale acct.	P	406
	inventory	P	425
Charles Henry	gdn. bond	P	84
Charles L.	will	T	330
Elizabeth	gdn. bond	R	146
	gdn. bond	S	171
Guy	admr. bond	Bond Bk.	138
Guy	gdn. bond	R	146
	gdn. acct.	S	171
	gdn. bond	S	457
John C.	gdn. bond	R	146
	gdn. acct.	S	171
	gdn. bond	S	457
Sarah Ann	will	I	394
	est. acct.	K	219
	inventory	K	275
	est. acct.	L	68
	(Sarah Ann Harris)		

Name	Document	Will Book	Page

BROADWATER (continued)

Thomas	gdn. bond	R	146
	gdn. acct.	S	171
	gdn. bond	S	457
William	gdn. bond	I	42
William E.	gdn. bond	K	26
	gdn. acct.	K	112

BRONAUGH

Agnes	admr. bond	A1 pt. 1	97
	inventory	A1 pt. 1	108, 212
David	admr. bond	A1 pt. 1	73
	est. acct.	A1 pt. 1	153
Elizabeth	inventory	B	363
	admr. bond	Bond Bk.	69
George	admr. bond	A1 pt. 2	356
	inventory	A1 pt. 2	366
	est. acct.	A1 pt. 2	402
	sale acct.	A1 pt. 2	403
Henry	admr. bond	F	225
Jeremiah	inventory	A1 pt. 1	82
	est. acct.	A1 pt. 1	152
	admr. bond	A1 pt. 2	317
	inventory	A1 pt. 2	406
	est. acct.	B	36
John	admr. bond	A1 pt. 1	122
	inventory	A1 pt. 1	135
	est. acct.	A1 pt. 2	402
Martin	inventory	Q	291
	sale acct.	Q	293
	est. acct.	R	115
Simpha Rosa	will	B	315
Ann Field	(a.k.a. Rosa Ann Field)		
	inventory	B	332

Name	Document	Will Book	Page
BRONAUGH (continued)			
William	admr. bond	Bond Bk.	144
	inventory	C	232*
	sale acct.	C	233*
	inventory	D	152
	est. acct.	D	154
BROOKE			
Benjamin M.	will	N	28
Sarah	gdn. bond	E	333
Walter	inventory	G	398
Walter D.	gdn. bond	H	33
	inventory	K	179
Walter D.'s heirs	gdn. bond	L	214
BROOKS			
Josiah	inventory	A1 pt. 2	498, 523
	est. acct.	B	66
BROOKSHIRE			
Sarah	inventory	A1 pt. 2	514
	est. acct.	A1 pt. 2	515
BROWN			
Anthony	inventory	P	401
	sale acct.	P	404
Catharine	will	K	140
Coleman	will	P	405
Daniel M.	inventory	G	228
Elizabeth	will	T	201
	inventory	U	244
	sale acct.	U	246
	div. of slaves	U	249
	est. acct.	U	415
Grace	will	D	407
James	admr. bond	A1 pt. 1	147
	inventory	B	39, 46
James	admr. bond	Bond Bk.	10

Name	Document	Will Book	Page
BROWN (continued)			
John	admr. bond	A1 pt. 1	92
	inventory	A1 pt. 1	99
	est. acct.	A1 pt. 1	101, 109
John	admr. bond	A1 pt. 1	240
	inventory	A1 pt. 1	245
	est. acct.	A1 pt. 1	246
	est. acct.	B	16
Richard	will	A1 pt. 1	110
	exor. bond	A1 pt. 1	112
	inventory	A1 pt. 1	115
William	admr. bond	Bond Bk.	167
Windsor	inventory	E	98
BROWNLEY			
Thomas	inventory	D	45
BRUESTER			
William	inventory	A1 pt. 2	542
BRUESTER see also BREWSTER			
BRUIN			
John	est. acct.	O	263
BRUMLEY			
Margaret	admr. bond	A1 pt. 2	306
	inventory	A1 pt. 2	353
	est. acct.	A1 pt. 2	354
BRUMMIT			
John	admr. bond	A1 pt. 1	198
	inventory	A1 pt. 1	204
BRUSTON			
Thomas	will	B	101
	inventory	B	107

Name	Document	Will Book	Page
BRYANT			
Philip	admr. bond	A1 pt. 2	420
	inventory	A1 pt. 2	465
BRYCE			
John	inventory	E	202
	sale acct.	E	205
BUCHANAN			
Elizabeth	will	D	267
	inventory	D	288
	admr. bond	Bond Bk.	183
BUCKLEY			
Annanias	gdn. bond	O	198
Catharine	gdn. bond	L	3
Harriet Ann	gdn. bond	O	198
James	admr. bond	F	234
	inventory	F	264
Jane	gdn. bond	O	198
Jane	will	X	403
John	will	I	250
John	gdn. bond	O	198
John H.	inventory	N	227
	sale acct.	O	214
	est. acct.	O	419
	est. acct.	P	159
Joshua	will	M	249
	inventory	M	276
	inventory	N	61
	slave inventory	N	63
	est. acct.	O	245
Joshua (elder)	est. acct.	O	267
Nimrod	inventory	N	22
	sale acct.	N	24
William	inventory	I	22
	est. acct.	L	9

Name	Document	Will Book	Page
BUCKNER			
Peyton	admr. bond	A1 pt. 2	424
	inventory	A1 pt. 2	499
BURDITT			
William T.	inventory	H	31
BURKE			
James	will	O	131
	inventory	O	199
	sale acct.	O	202
	est. acct.	P	167
	sale acct.	R	197, 357
	est. acct.	S	304
John	est. acct.	Q	77
John B.	est. acct.	O	242
	est. acct.	P	170
Silas	inventory	X	406
BURN			
Daniel	will	A1 pt. 2	435
	inventory	A1 pt. 2	470
James	admr. bond	A1 pt. 2	431
	inventory	A1 pt. 2	434

BURN see also BYRN

Name	Document	Will Book	Page
BURNHAM			
Raymond	inventory	D	55
	sale acct.	D	90
	est. acct.	D	91
	admr. bond	Bond Bk.	161
BURRE			
Nancy	gdn. bond	E	243

Name	Document	Will Book	Page
BURSTON			
William	admr. bond	A1 pt. 1	187
	inventory	A1 pt. 1	195
	est. acct.	A1 pt. 1	221
BURTON			
Benjamin	will	K	227*
	inventory	K	229
	curator bond	K	228, 230
	inventory	L	92*
BUSHBY			
William	will (1810 - Washington Co. - see FDBs V2:189 & Y2:134)		
BUTCHER			
Eleanor	inventory	B	15
John	admr. bond	G	315
	inventory	G	317
BUTLER			
John	est. acct.	R	302
	est. acct.*		
Kitty Maria	gdn. bond	N	39
William C. B.	will	R	58
	inventory	R	185
	sale acct.	R	189
	est. acct.	R	261
	est. acct.	S	202, 501
	est. acct.	T	161
BYRN			
Patrick	admr. bond	Bond Bk.	66

BYRN see also BURN

Name	Document	Will Book	Page
CALVERT			
George	will	Q	63
	inventory	Q	278
	est. acct.	U	7
Priscilla	will	U	29
CAMPBELL			
John	acct.	A1 pt. 2	296
John	gdn. bond	K	304
CANADY			
John	admr. bond	Bond Bk.	81
CANADY see also **KENNEDY**			
CANTERBURY			
Ruth	admr. bond	A1 pt. 2	360
Samuel	will	B	370
	inventory	B	371
	est. acct.	C	17, 61, 183
CARFORD			
Samuel	will	A1 pt. 2	518
	inventory	A1 pt. 2	522
	est. acct.	B	14
CARLYLE			
John	will	D	203
	inventory	D	368
	account with Carlyle & Dalton	E	416, 418, 420
	est. acct.	L	31
CARNEY			
Thomas	admr. bond	A1 pt. 1	96
	inventory	A1 pt. 1	106
	est. acct.	A1 pt. 1	120

Name	Document	Will Book	Page
CAROLIN			
John	inventory	I	269
	est. acct.	K	88
CARPENTER			
Richard	exor. bond	A1 pt. 2	430
	will	A1 pt. 2	431
	inventory	A1 pt. 2	489
CARPER			
Catharine L.	gdn. bond	U	443
Francis E.	gdn. bond	U	443
Frederick	committee bond	U	172
	inventory	V	30
	sale acct.	V	33
	committee acct.	V	173
Philip W.	gdn. bond	U	443
Thomas E.	gdn. bond	U	443
CARRINGTON			
Eli	will	N	41
	inventory	O	268
	sale acct.	O	269
Nancy	inventory	N	56
	sale acct.	N	77
	est. acct.	R	106
Timothy	est. acct.	R	105
CARROLL			
Charles Jr.	admr. bond	Bond Bk.	122
Daniel	inventory	E	231
Dempsey	will (1776 - Loudoun Co. WB B:132)		
John	inventory	N	332
	est. acct.	O	292
Joseph	est. acct.	B	405
	admr. bond	Bond Bk.	68
Nicholas	admr. bond	A1 pt. 1	148
	inventory	A1 pt. 1	151

Name	Document	Will Book	Page
CARSON			
Thomas	will	C	153
CARTER			
Charles B.'s children	gdn. acct.	M	184, 189
Elizabeth L.	gdn. bond	M	126
	gdn. acct.	M	184, 189
	gdn. acct.	Q	128
Elizabeth L.	will	X	385
Emily H.	gdn. bond	K	61
	gdn. bond	L	155*
Jane	inventory	L	69
Janet	will	I	443
John F. Sr.	will	I	30
	inventory	I	69
	est. acct.	I	159
	sale acct.	I	333
	est. acct.	J	37
	sale acct.	J	94
John Hill	gdn. acct.	M	184, 189
Mary W.	gdn. bond	M	126
	gdn. acct.	M	184, 189
	gdn. acct.	Q	128
Robert	committee bond	J	164
	est. acct.	K	101
Robert (of Baltimore)	will (partial)	PLC#2	127
Susan	gdn. acct.	M	184, 189
William Fitzhugh	will	S	70
Wormley	inventory	N	256
	sale acct.	N	258
	est. acct.	N	262
CARUTHERS			
James	admr. bond	A1 pt. 1	266

Name	Document	Will Book	Page
CASEY			
John	will	G	43
	exor. bond	G	45
	inventory	G	72
CASH			
Elijah	inventory	O	82
	sale acct.	O	84
	est. acct.	O	272
Joseph	inventory	I	397
William	inventory	L	183
	sale acct.	L	184
	est. acct.	N	208
CASHAT			
John	admr. bond	A1 pt. 1	257
	inventory	A1 pt. 2	282
CASTELLO			
Bridget	inventory	C	75
	est. acct.	C	76
	admr. bond	Bond Bk.	96
CAVENER			
John	will	B	87
	inventory	B	88
CHAMPNEYS			
William	will	A1 pt. 2	443
	inventory	A1 pt. 2	472
CHAPIN			
Benjamin	will	D	233
	inventory	D	419
Elizabeth	gdn. bond	E	170

Name	Document	Will Book	Page
CHAPMAN			
Constant	dower	B	339
	will (1774)	F	1
	will (1768)	G	359
Nathaniel	inventory	B	323, 325
	admr. bond	Bond Bk.	59
CHAPPELL			
John	will	R	329
	inventory	S	35
	sale acct	S	37
	est. acct.	T	99
Mary	inventory	X	25
	sale acct.	X	265, 308
	est. acct.	X	442
William H.	inventory	X	315
CHARLTON			
Andrew	inventory	B	166
	est. acct.	B	166
	admr. bond	Bond Bk.	31
CHESHIRE			
John	admr. bond	A1 pt. 1	239
	admr. bond	Bond Bk.	53
	est. acct.	B	2, 13, 22, 227
	inventory	B	218
CHEW			
Mercy	will	C	243
	sale acct.	D	72
	inventory	D	73
Roger	inventory	F	236
	sale acct.	F	241
	est. acct.	G	289
	div. of slaves	G	291

Name	Document	Will Book	Page
CHICHESTER			
Doddridge Pitt	admr. bond	Sup. Ct.	73
Richard	will	G	194
	codicil	G	211
	exor. bond	G	212
	inventory	G	273
	inventory (Fauquier Co.)	G	293
	est. acct.	K	93
William	gdn. bond	M	181
CHICK			
Rebecca	inventory	I	448
William	inventory	I	449
CHILDS			
Ann E.	gdn. bond	R	146
Benjamin	gdn. bond	J	230
Elizabeth	gdn. bond	J	230
Gabriel D.	will	J	151
	inventory	K	281
Gabriel D.	inventory	R	129
	sale acct.	R	130
	est. acct.	R	275
	est. acct.	S	163
Lewis H.	inventory	R	154
Margaret Ann	gdn. bond	R	153
Mary	gdn. bond	J	230
Nancy	gdn. bond	J	230
Samuel	gdn. bond	J	230
Sarah	gdn. bond	J	230
Wesley	gdn. bond	J	230
William	gdn. bond	J	230
CHURCH			
Thomas	will	J	35

Name	Document	Will Book	Page
CLAPHAM			
Josiah	will	A1 pt. 2	309
	exor. bond	A1 pt. 2	310
	inventory	A1 pt. 2	375
	est. acct.	B	26
CLARK(E)			
Aaron	inventory	C	256
	admr. bond	Bond Bk.	150
Ann	est. acct.	U	4
Belsasett	inventory	V	366
	sale acct.	V	371
Elizabeth	gdn. bond	G	263
Frances E.	gdn. bond	W	201
John	will	C	224
	inventory	C	231
John	will	E	183
	inventory	E	193
	est. acct.	G	282, 408
John P.	gdn. bond	G	263
Josiah	will	M	268
	inventory	M	411
	sale acct.	M	414
	est. acct.	O	203
	est. acct.	Q	260
Josiah M.	gdn. bond	L	402
Lucinda	gdn. bond	L	402
Richard	will	J	346
	inventory	J	389
Rose	will	E	180
Thompson	will	T	396
CLEARY			
Thomas Rieley	gdn. bond	W	79

Name	Document	Will Book	Page
CLEMENTS			
Charles	inventory	K	259
	sale acct.	N	273
	est. acct.	N	275
Mary	inventory	W	62
	sale acct.	W	64
	est. acct.	W	181
Polly	gdn. bond	K	328
CLEVELAND			
Johnston	will (1834 - Loudoun Co.)*		
CLIFTON			
Elizabeth	will	C	225
	inventory	C	233
Thomas	admr. bond	Bond Bk.	342
William	inventory	C	142
	admr. bond	Bond Bk.	112, 142
CLINE			
Matilda Ann B. see WEST, Matilda Ann B.			
COAKLEY			
James W.	will	V	23
	inventory	V	67
	est. acct.	W	12
COCKBURN			
Martin	will	L	403
	inventory	M	376
	inventory	N	137
COCKE			
William	inventory	B	190

Name	Document	Will Book	Page
COCKERILLE			
Americus	gdn. bond	R	132
	gdn. bond	T	123
	gdn. acct.	T	270
	gdn. acct.	U	157, 183b
	gdn. bond	U	172
	gdn. acct.	W	103
Ann	will	U	356
	est. acct.	W	101
	sale acct. & est. acct.*		
Behethlean	div. of est.	S	5
Elizabeth	trustee acct.	U	109
Florida	gdn. bond	T	123
	gdn. acct.	U	157, 183b
	gdn. bond	U	172
	gdn. acct.	W	103
George	will	K	268
Henry	gdn. bond	K	2
Hannah Frances	gdn. bond	R	132
	gdn. bond	T	123
	gdn. acct.	T	270
	gdn. acct.	U	157, 183b
	gdn. bond	U	172
	gdn. acct.	W	103
James C.	gdn. bond	R	132
	gdn. bond	T	123
	gdn. acct.	T	270
	gdn. acct.	U	157, 183b
	gdn. bond	U	172
	gdn. acct.	W	103
Jane Behethlin	will	O	111
	inventory	P	147
Jeremiah	will	J	152
	inventory	J	157
Joseph	will	G	92
	exor. bond	G	102
	admr. bond	G	176

Name	Document	Will Book	Page
COCKERILLE (continued)			
Lucy Ellen	gdn. bond	T	123
	gdn. acct.	U	157, 183b
	gdn. bond	U	172
	gdn. acct.	W	103
Mary Ellen	gdn. bond	U	336
	gdn. bond	V	392
Mottrom	inventory	P	120
	sale acct.	P	122
	est. acct.	P	155, 270
	est. acct.	Q	119
Nancy	committee bond	U	336
Richard	gdn. bond	K	2
Richard H.	sale acct.	T	315
	inventory	T	321
	est. acct.	U	4, 201
Richard H.'s children	gdn. acct.	T	270
Sampson	will	F	5
	exor. bond	F	7
	inventory	F	42
	est. acct.	J	232
Samuel J.	gdn. bond	R	132
	gdn. bond	T	123
	gdn. acct.	T	270
	gdn. acct.	U	157, 183b
	gdn. bond	U	172
	gdn. acct.	W	103
Sandford	inventory	V	95
	sale acct.	V	101
Sarah	will	N	136
Seth	gdn. bond	R	132
	gdn. bond	T	123
	gdn. acct.	T	270
	gdn. acct.	U	157, 183b
	gdn. bond	U	172
	gdn. acct.	W	103

Name	Document	Will Book	Page
COCKERILLE (continued)			
Thomas	inventory	L	223
	sale acct.	M	2
COE			
William	exor. bond	F	228
	will	F	230
	inventory	F	267
COFFER			
Francis	admr. bond	A1 pt. 1	58
	est. acct.	S	194
Francis	will	L	156*
	est. acct.	S	194
John	will	J	146
	inventory	K	348
	est. acct.	K	379
	est. acct.	M	100
	est. acct.	P	317
Joshua	inventory	K	70
	sale acct.	K	72
	div. of slaves	K	74
	est. acct.	K	106, 224
Mary	sale acct.	L	325
	est. acct.	L	326
Thomas	gdn. bond	K	205
Thomas Withers	will	D	260
	inventory	E	241
COHAGEN			
Michael	admr. bond	F	256
COHEN			
Jacob	will	G	391

Name	Document	Will Book	Page
COLCLOUGH			
Benjamin	will	D	301
	inventory	D	302
	est. acct.	D	304
COLE			
William	admr. bond	Bond Bk.	174
COLEMAN			
Ann Caroline	gdn. bond	R	338
Charles	gdn. bond	K	361
Charles	will	P	229
Charles Thomas	gdn. bond	R	338
	adv.Turley-decree	T	302
George W.	will	U	125
George William	gdn. bond	R	338
	gdn. bond	V	215
	adv.Turley-decree	T	302
James	gdn. bond	L	179
James	will	L	122
	inventory	M	48
	est. acct.	N	101
	est. acct.	O	321
	est. acct.	P	29
John	will	K	338
	inventory	L	11
Johnson J.	will	R	81
	inventory	S	268
Patsy	dower	T	125
	inventory	V	309
	sale acct.	V	314
	est. acct.	X	153
Richard	est. acct.	U	74
	adv.Turley-decree	T	302
	admr. bond	Sup. Ct.	71
	est. acct.	Sup. Ct.	100, 113

Name	Document	Will Book	Page
COLEMAN (continued)			
Richard J.	inventory	Q	421
	sale acct.	R	1
	est. acct.	R	61
Samuel	est. acct.	W	64
Sarah	will	V	146
COLLARD			
Margaret	will	X	317
Samuel	inventory	E	142
Samuel	will	W	281
COLLINS			
James	admr. bond	I	12
COLVILL(E)			
Francis	will	C	148
John	will	B	97
	inventory	B	135, 141
	est. acct.	B	395, 442
	est. acct.	E	334
	est. acct.	E	280, 282
Thomas	will	B	424*
	inventory	C	144
	est. acct.	E	338, 376
	est. acct.	F	278, 283, 284
	est. acct.	G	118
COMER			
Dennis	will	W	319
	inventory	W	367*
	sale acct.	X	23
	est. acct.	X	54*
Elias	gdn. bond	U	154
Jane Catharine	gdn. bond	U	154

Name	Document	Will Book	Page
COMER (continued)			
John	will	S	469
	inventory	T	111
	sale acct.	T	113
	est. acct.	T	264
	est. acct.	V	156
Michael	admr. bond	Bond Bk.	157
Silas	gdn. bond	U	154
COMPTON			
Albert	gdn. bond	L	417
Betsy	gdn. bond	L	417
Elijah	gdn. bond	L	417
John	admr. bond	A1 pt. 1	159
	inventory	A1 pt. 1	178
	est. acct.	B	63
John	inventory	L	152*
	admr. bond	L	307
John	gdn. bond	L	417
John P.	admr. bond	G	268
	inventory	H	88
Ludwell	est. acct.	X	429
Rhoda	gdn. bond	L	417
Varnell	est. acct.	M	141
William	gdn. bond	L	417
CONN			
Hugh	will	I	524
	inventory	J	182
Jesse	will	W	156
CONNELL			
James	will	D	9
	est. acct.	D	241
Simon	will	A1 pt. 1	87
	exor. bond	A1 pt. 1	89
	inventory	A1 pt. 1	94

Name	Document	Will Book	Page
CONWAY			
Richard	will	J	113
COOK(E)			
Edward	admr. bond	A1 pt. 2	284
	inventory	A1 pt. 2	323
Elizabeth P.	gdn. bond	R	87
George W.	gdn. bond	R	87
	gdn. acct.	V	334
Giles	will	I	531
Giles F.	will	R	329
John	gdn. bond	R	87
Mary T.	gdn. bond	R	87
Whiting	inventory	P	393
William	gdn. bond	R	87
COOKSEY			
Francis A.	gdn. bond	U	243
Isabella	gdn. bond	U	243
COOMES			
Catharine	will	B	67
	inventory	B	84
COOPER			
Joel	will	E	126
	inventory	E	131
Joseph	gdn. bond	T	218
COPPER			
Cyrus	inventory	E	381
CORNISH			
Charles	will	C	235
	inventory	C	238
Elizabeth	will	C	253

Name	Document	Will Book	Page
CORSE			
John	will	U	347
COULTER			
Peter	will	P	242
	inventory	Q	27
	sale acct.	Q	337
	inventory	S	229
	sale acct.	S	231
	est. acct.	T	46
COWARD			
Ann	renounces provisions of husband		
	John's will	Q	128
John	will	Q	127
	inventory	R	139
	sale acct.	R	141
	est. acct.	R	270, 272
COX			
Elizabeth	will	F	173
	exor. bond	F	175
Presley	inventory	D	394
	est. acct.	E	22
	admr. bond	Bond Bk.	182
Sally	admr. bond	Sup. Ct.	129
COYLE			
Michael	will	C	221
CRAGUE see CRAIG			
CRAIG			
David	inventory	B	237
	est. acct.	B	390
	admr. bond	Bond Bk.	56
Paul	admr. bond	A1 pt. 2	270
	inventory	A1 pt. 2	291

Name	Document	Will Book	Page
CRAIG (continued)			
Samuel	will	J	191
	list of debts	J	271
CRAIK(E)			
George W.	will (1808 - Alexandria -		
	see FDB O2:175)		
James	will	K	180
	inventory	L	158*
James	gdn. bond	K	293
	gdn. bond	M	68
	gdn. acct.	O	138
CRAN(D)FORD			
Elizabeth	gdn. bond	U	115, 135
Emily	gdn. bond	U	115, 135
James Lucian	gdn. bond	U	115, 135
John	inventory	S	77
	sale acct.	S	80
	admr. bond	Sup. Ct.	113
William J.	will	S	91
CREASE			
Anthony	will	M	280
CRITCHER			
Jadwin	will	A1 pt. 2	342
	exor. bond	A1 pt. 2	343
	inventory	A1 pt. 2	376
	est. acct.	B	44
CROSON			
Thomas	est. acct.	O	271
	admr. bond	Sup. Ct.	58
CROSS			
John	will	J	402
Mary	will	L	182

Name	Document	Will Book	Page
CROSSTHWAITE			
Anthony	will	C	107
	inventory	C	115
CRUMP			
George	will	V	50
CULVERHOUSE			
John	admr. bond	A1 pt. 1	142
	inventory	A1 pt. 1	143
CUMMINS			
King	inventory	W	307
	sale acct.	W	309
	est. acct.	X	420
CUNNINGHAM			
William	exor. bond	G	296
	will	G	297
	est. acct.	G	392
CURRY			
Barnaby	inventory	B	144
	est. acct.	B	211
	admr. bond	Bond Bk.	36
CURTIS			
David	inventory	V	140
Elizabeth	will	W	120
CUSSEE			
Margaret	gdn. bond	G	139
CUSTIS			
Eleanor P.	gdn. bond	G	420
	gdn. acct.	I	286, 299

Name	Document	Will Book	Page
CUSTIS (continued)			
Elizabeth P.	gdn. bond	G	46
	disbursement	G	462, 465
	gdn. bond	I	286
George W. P.	disbursement	G	453, 472
	gdn. acct.	I	289, 299
	gdn. acct.	K	122
John Park	inventory	D	274
	inventory	E	11, 14, 17
	est. acct.	G	149, 156, 323
	est. acct.	I	280
	est. acct.	K	124
	admr. bond	Bond Bk.	179
Martha (Patsy)	gdn. bond	G	46
	disbursement	G	464, 465
	gdn. acct.	I	283
	gdn. acct.	K	121
DADE			
Catharine	admr. bond	F	133
Francis	admr. bond	Bond Bk.	140, 169
Langhorne	gdn. bond	K	187
	gdn. acct.	K	343
Nancy	gdn. bond	K	187
	gdn. acct.	K	343
Townshend	will	D	234
DAILY			
Timothy	inventory	P	248
	sale acct.	P	250
	est. acct.	P	295

DAILY see also DAYLY

DALTON			
John	will	D	17
	inventory	E	300, 311
Robert	admr. bond	F	50

Name	Document	Will Book	Page
DANCE			
John	will	G	379
DANIEL, John O. see O'DANIEL, John			
DANIEL			
Stephen	will	X	183
	inventory	X	329
	sale acct.	X	331
DARBY			
Elizabeth	inventory	I	446
	est. acct.	M	219, 228
DARNE			
Amelia B.	inventory	W	3
	sale acct.	W	5
	est. acct.	W	320*
Ann A.	gdn. bond	W	117
Henry	will	I	510
	inventory	I	525
	div. of slaves	J	253
	est. acct.	J	330
	sale acct.	K	340
	est. acct.	K	342
John	will	M	181
	inventory	M	193
Mary	inventory	N	279
	sale acct.	N	281
	est. acct.	O	238
Nicholas	will	T	172
	inventory	T	213
	sale acct.	T	217*
	sale acct.	W	6
	est. acct.	W	322*
Penelope	will	K	236
William	will	J	163

Name	Document	Will Book	Page
DARRELL			
Augustus	will	D	3*
	inventory	D	97
	est. acct.	D	207
Cordelia	will	D	416
George	will	C	108*
	inventory	C	120
	est. acct.	C	247
Mary	will	G	69
	exor. bond	G	79
	inventory	G	107
	est. acct.	G	109
Sampson	will	D	40*
Sarah	admr. bond	Bond Bk.	129
William	will	G	393
	inventory	H	127
	est. acct.	I	1, 358
	est. acct.	J	205, 281
	est. acct.	K	156
DAUGHERTY			
Constant	admr. bond	Bond Bk.	159a
DAVIS			
Adam	will	X	263
Aquilla I.	inventory	X	390
	sale acct.	X	392
Attoway R.	vs. Davis' admr.	O	1, 4
Benjamin	inventory	B	321
	admr. bond	Bond Bk.	64
Benjamin	will	K	115
Benjamin R.	will	M	288
	inventory of slaves	O	2
	est. acct.	O	379
Benjamin R.'s admr.	adv. Jane Davis, etc.	O	1
Chloe	gdn. bond	G	179

Name	Document	Will Book	Page
DAVIS (continued)			
Edward	admr. bond	Bond Bk.	101
	inventory	C	76
Edward	sale acct.	J	397
	inventory	J	404
Elenor	will	V	308
Frances M.	gdn. bond	V	313
Harriet	gdn. bond	N	297
Isaac	admr. bond	F	326
	inventory	G	18
	est. acct.	G	132
Jane	vs. Davis' admr.	O	1
Jemima	gdn. bond	G	95
John	will	N	106
Julia A.	trustee acct.	S	495
Lucinda R.	gdn. bond	N	209
	vs. Davis' admr.	O	1
	gdn. acct.	S	314
Mary	gdn. bond	N	136, 297
	gdn. acct.	R	311, 313
Nehemiah	will	H	78
Nehemiah	gdn. bond	M	297
Nehemiah R.	vs. Davis' admr.	O	1
Newman	gdn. bond	N	310
Norman R.	gdn. bond	N	209
	vs. Davis' admr.	O	1
	gdn. bond	R	333
Peggy R.	gdn. bond	N	209
	vs. Davis' admr.	O	1
Peter	admr. bond	H	206
Priscilla	will	N	296
Rezin	gdn. bond	N	310
Richard S.	est. acct.	R	280
Simon R.	gdn. bond	N	209
	vs. Davis' admr.	O	1
	gdn. bond	S	82
	gdn. acct.	S	207

Name	Document	Will Book	Page
DAVIS (continued)			
Simon R. (cont'd)	gdn. bond	S	217
Simpson	gdn. bond	N	310
Susanna	gdn. bond	E	362
Thomas	will	B	151
	inventory	B	180
Virginia F.	will (1835 - Frederick Co.)*		
William R.	inventory	X	202*
	sale acct.	X	300
	est. acct.	X	431
DAYLY			
Hugh	admr. bond	Bond Bk.	147
DAYLY see also **DAILY**			
DEAGAN			
Henry B.	will	P	39
DEAKIN			
Francis	will	I	431
William	will	I	426
DEAN			
Joseph	will	L	215
DEAVERS			
Lewis	gdn. bond	T	352
	gdn. bond	U	326*
DEBELL			
Elizabeth	inventory	U	265*
John	inventory	B	83
	admr. bond	Bond Bk.	3
John	will	U	337
	est. acct.	X	133
John T.	gdn. bond	U	370

Name	Document	Will Book	Page
DEBELL (continued)			
Mary E.	gdn. bond	U	370
William	will	K	249
	inventory	L	75
	sale acct.	L	377
	est. acct.	L	379
DEMING			
Philip E.	inventory	X	80
	(Rappahannock Co.)		
	inventory (Fairfax)	X	87
	sale acct. (Fairfax)	X	94
	sale acct.	X	109
	(Rappahannock Co.)		
DENEALE			
Edward	inventory	H	153
	sale acct.	I	268
	est. acct.	I	272, 277
George	gdn. bond	H	34
James	will	I	533
	inventory	J	51
	sale acct.	J	82
	est. acct.	J	86
James	inventory	Q	21
	sale acct.	Q	22
John E.	gdn. bond	K	241
	gdn. acct.	L	132*
	gdn. bond	L	245
	gdn. acct.	L	332
Sybil	gdn. bond	K	237
	gdn. bond	L	219
	gdn. acct.	M	71
	gdn. bond	M	74
William	will	K	233*
	inventory order	K	293
	sale acct.	K	417

Name	Document	Will Book	Page
DENEALE (continued)			
William (cont'd)	est. acct.	L	3
	est. acct.	M	92
	est. acct.	p	60
DENNEY			
Edmund	inventory	L	279
DENT			
George	inventory	B	177
	admr. bond	Bond Bk.	45
Thomas	will	A1 pt. 2	460
	inventory	A1 pt. 2	482, 485
DENTY			
Jonathan	will	J	401
	inventory	K	31
DEVAUGHN			
Thomas	admr. bond	F	225
DEVERS see DEAVERS			
DEVIN			
James	exor. bond	A1 pt. 2	418
	will	A1 pt. 2	419
	inventory	A1 pt. 2	464
DEWEY			
James	est. acct.	I	156
DICK			
Elisha C.	will	O	53
	inventory	O	152
	sale acct.	O	155
Sarah S.	est. acct.	V	291

Name	Document	Will Book	Page
DICKEY			
James	will	K	222
William	inventory	I	313
	est. acct.	I	364
DISNEY			
Cornelius	gdn. bond	V	322
Edward	gdn. bond	V	322
George	gdn. bond	V	322
John	inventory	V	51
	sale acct.	V	54
John B.	est. acct.	X	60
John W.	gdn. bond	V	7
Juliet(te)	gdn. bond	V	322
Mary Jane	gdn. bond	V	7
Richard	gdn. bond	V	7
Robert	gdn. bond	V	7
Samuel	gdn. bond	V	322
DODSON			
Ann	dower allotted	Q	21
Charles	will	I	393
	inventory	J	234
	inventory	K	321
	est. acct.	K	400
	est. acct.	Q	75
Thomas	inventory	Q	18
	sale acct.	Q	20
	est. acct.	Q	205
DOGIN			
John	will	C	109
	inventory	C	121
DONALDSON			
James	will	C	90
	inventory	C	96

Name	Document	Will Book	Page

DONALDSON (continued)

James	admr. bond	F	47
	inventory	F	128
	division	F	130
James	gdn. bond	R	131
William	est. acct.	B	272
	inventory	C	41
	admr. bond	Bond Bk.	91
William	will	L	94*
William Jr.	admr. bond	Bond Bk.	22

DOROTHY

Constantine	see DOUGHERTY, Constantine	

DORSEY

Hester Lorinda	gdn. bond	S	69
	gdn. acct.	S	527
	gdn. acct.	T	354
James	inventory	N	363
	sale acct.	O	197
	est. acct.	O	324
	est. acct.	P	264
Lorinda	see DORSEY, Hester Lorinda		
Margaret	gdn. bond	S	69
	gdn. acct.	S	527
	gdn. acct.	T	353
	gdn. acct.	U	161, 230

DOUGHERTY

Constantine	inventory	D	46

DOUGLASS

Jacob	exor. bond	A1 pt. 2	357
	will	A1 pt. 2	358
James Jr.	admr. bond	G	41
	inventory	G	116
	est. acct.	G	125

Name	Document	Will Book	Page
DOUGLASS (Continued)			
Robert	admr. bond	Bond Bk.	98
Robert H.	gdn. bond	J	98
DOW(E)			
Alexander	will	K	256
	inventory	L	163*
	sale acct.	L	165
	est. acct.	O	275
DOWDALL			
Thomas	will	C	104
	inventory	C	118
DRANE			
Washington	est. acct.	R	60
	inventory	R	248
DRAPER			
Catharine	gdn. bond	T	81
Eliza M.	gdn. bond	T	81
Maria Louisa	gdn. bond	T	81
Simeon	inventory	R	204
	sale acct.	R	207
	admr. bond	Sup. Ct.	69, 70
	est. acct.	Sup. Ct.	122
DUCKER			
John	will	A1 pt. 1	215
	inventory	A1 pt. 1	216
	exor. bond	A1 pt. 1	225
	est. acct.	A1 pt. 1	241
DULANY			
Henry G.	gdn. acct.	V	194

Name	Document	Will Book	Page
DULANY (continued)			
Henry R.	will	T	79
	est. acct.	U	59
	inventory	U	360
	est. acct.	V	182, 279
Henry R.	gdn. bond	T	300
	gdn. acct.	W	372
Martin	admr. bond	A1 pt. 2	312
	inventory	A1 pt. 2	441
Rebecca A.	gdn. acct.	V	187
	gdn. acct.	X	1*
DULIN			
Edward	will	D	298
	inventory	D	328
Edward	gdn. bond	D	305
	gdn. acct.	E	174
Elizabeth	inventory	B	255
	est. acct.	B	317
	admr. bond	Bond Bk.	58
John	gdn. bond	D	305
	gdn. acct.	E	177
John	will	F	39
	exor. bond	F	49
	inventory	F	67
Sarah	will	H	170
Susanna	est. acct.	S	526
	est. acct.	T	149
William	will	B	149
	inventory	B	169
	est. acct.	B	176
DUNCAN			
Blanchflower	inventory	B	75
	admr. bond	Bond Bk.	20
George	will	E	3

Name	Document	Will Book	Page
DUNDASS			
John	will (1813 - Alexandria)		
DUREY			
James	inventory	H	242
DUTY			
Thomas	inventory	J	392
DYE			
Daniel	inventory	Q	285
	sale acct.	Q	294
	est. acct.	S	444
Emily	gdn. bond	R	341
Frances Virginia	gdn. bond	V	74
Henry C.	gdn. bond	R	341
Huldah	gdn. bond	R	341
James	gdn. bond	V	74
John	gdn. bond	V	74
John H.	will	O	371
	inventory	P	125
	sale acct.	P	132
Mary	inventory	Q	283
	sale acct.	Q	294
	est. acct.	S	445
Mary	gdn. bond	R	341
DYER			
Zachariah	will	T	366
DYSON			
Ellen M.	gdn. bond	V	391
EARNSHAW			
John	admr. bond	E	341
John	inventory	N	213
	sale acct.	N	216
	est. acct.	P	374, 378
	est. acct.	Q	201

Name	Document	Will Book	Page
EARP(E)			
Caleb	will	H	193
	admr. bond	H	194
John	admr. bond	A1 pt. 1	95
	inventory	A1 pt. 1	106
	est. acct.	A1 pt. 1	133
Joshua	inventory	A1 pt. 2	478
	est. acct.	B	43
Joseph	inventory	C	122
	admr. bond	Bond Bk.	111
William	admr. bond	A1 pt. 1	267
	inventory	A1 pt. 2	307
	est. acct.	A1 pt. 2	308
ELGIN			
Catharine S.	gdn. bond	U	262*
Eliza R.	gdn. bond	U	262
Gustavus A.	inventory	U	385
	sale acct.	U	386
	est. acct.	W	360*
Hamilton	inventory	Q	232
	sale acct.	Q	324
	est. acct.	T	31
ELIASON			
William A.	will	T	96
ELLIOTT			
James	will	I	180
	inventory	I	305
ELLZEY			
Francis	will	A1 pt. 2	461
Lewis	will	E	223*
	inventory	E	245
	admr. bond	G	24
	est. acct.	N	269

Name	Document	Will Book	Page
ELLZEY (continued)			
Mary	will	F	70
	exor. bond	F	72
Thomas	admr. bond	A1 pt. 1	37
	inventory	A1 pt. 1	49
	est. acct.	A1 pt. 1	223
Thomazin	inventory	L	191
	est. acct.	P	262, 310
	sale acct. (land)	Q	112
	est. acct.	Q	114, 149, 319
	est. acct.	S	322
ELTON			
John	will	E	27
	inventory	E	33
EMERSON			
William	inventory	O	329
ENGLISH			
Edmond	will	A1 pt. 1	127
	exor. bond	A1 pt. 1	128
	inventory	A1 pt. 1	141
Walter	admr. bond	Bond Bk.	48
ESKRIDGE			
Charles	will	I	308
	inventory	I	370
ESTES			
H. S.	div. of slaves	M	69
EVANS			
David	will (1771 - Philadelphia, Pa. - see FDB V2:241)		
Griffith	will (1767 - Philadelphia, Pa. - see FDB V2:241)		

Name	Document	Will Book	Page
EVANS (continued)			
John	will (1766 - Loudoun Co. - see FDB V2:241)		
John	will	A1 pt. 1	211
	admr. bond	A1 pt. 1	214
	inventory	A1 pt. 1	216
	inventory	A1 pt. 2	509
	est. acct.	B	201
John	admr. bond	G	111
	inventory	G	126
	admr. bond	I	10
	inventory	I	66
John	gdn. bond	I	152
Thomas	inventory	A1 pt. 2	503
	est. acct.	B	240
William	gdn. bond	I	152
EWEN			
Patrick	admr. bond	F	258
FAIRFAX			
Albert	sale acct.(see CFF#3p - Bank of Alexandria vs. Albert Fairfax- 1834)		
Ann	est. divided	G	294
Ann	gdn. bond	I	215
Bryan	will	I	150
Ferdinando	will	M	143
Henry	will	V	121
	inventory	V	142
	sale acct.	V	145
Jane	will	I	418
Sally Cary	will (1811 - Orphans Court, Alexandria)		
Sarah	est. acct.	G	294
Sanford	est. acct.	Z	261*
Thomas	will	U	382
	est. acct.	X	205, 211, 217

Name	Document	Will Book	Page

FAIRFAX (continued)

William	will	B	171*
	inventory	B	206

FALLEN

Agatha	will	F	125

FALLEN see also FOLLIN

FARGUSON

John	see FERGUSON, John	

FARR

Ann M.	will	X	402
Elizabeth	adv. Davis' admr.	O	1
Matilda	sale acct.	R	364
Nicholas	will	W	201
Peggy	gdn. bond	I	386
Rezin	gdn. bond	Sup. Ct.	135
Richard	gdn. bond	R	138
	gdn. bond	Sup. Ct.	135
Richard R.	will	U	330
	est. acct.	W	335*
Roger	gdn. bond	L	218
Roger W.	est. acct.(see CFF#30o -		
	Farr vs. Farr's admr. - 1835)		
	children gdn. bond	R	251
Samuel	inventory	J	387
	est. acct.	O	334

FAULKNER

William	inventory	X	386

FENLEY

Charles B.	will	E	324
	exor. bond	E	325
Walter	inventory	E	272

Name	Document	Will Book	Page

FENLEY see also **FINLEY**

FERGUSON

Name	Document	Will Book	Page
James	gdn. bond	E	340
John	will	B	245
	inventory	B	263
	est. acct.	B	357
	est. acct.	J	352
Joshua	will	C	78
	inventory	C	81
	est. acct.	C	85
Joshua	inventory	J	395
	est. acct.	K	195
	sale acct.	K	197

FIELDS

Name	Document	Will Book	Page
Simon	inventory	T	175
	sale acct.	T	177

FINCH

Name	Document	Will Book	Page
Mary	admr. bond	Sup. Ct.	52

FINLAY see **FINLEY**

FINLEY

Name	Document	Will Book	Page
David	admr. bond	F	296
	inventory	G	56
John B.	will	J	221
	inventory	J	251, 421

FINLEY see also **FENLEY**

FINNACUM

Name	Document	Will Book	Page
Benjamin	inventory	Q	243
	sale acct.	Q	244

Name	Document	Will Book	Page
FISH			
Elizabeth	est. acct.	U	305
Francis	will	P	116
	inventory	P	142
	inventory	U	255*
	sale acct.	U	256
	est. acct.	U	305
FISHER			
Amos	inventory	I	244
	sale acct.	I	247
FITZGERALD			
John	will	H	56
	inventory	I	15, 19
	est. acct.	I	49, 108, 318, 324, 329
	sale acct.	I	325
	exr. acct.	O	178
FITZHUGH			
Andrew	inventory	W	90, 94
	est. acct.	W	266
Harrison	gdn. bond	K	376
Henry	will (1783 - King George Co.)		
John	gdn. bond	J	393
	inventory	K	24
	gdn. bond	K	168
	gdn. acct.	K	153, 208
	gdn. acct.	L	103
	gdn. bond	L	396
	gdn. acct.	M	93, 388, 396
Mead(e)	will	U	328*
	est. acct.	V	180
Nancy F.	gdn. bond	N	135
Nathaniel	will	H	151
	admr. bond	H	242

Name	Document	Will Book	Page
FITZHUGH (continued)			
Nathaniel (cont'd)	inventory	I	350
	est. acct.	I	492
	est. acct.	L	188
Nicholas	will	K	283
	est. acct.	L	308
	inventory	L	358
	div. of slaves	M	235
Nicholas	will	R	227
Richard	will	M	240
	inventory	M	246
	est. acct.	M	409
	est. acct.	P	189
Sarah	inventory	J	201
Sarah	will	R	242
(of King George Co.)			
Thomas	will (1829 - Prince William Co.)*		
William	will	J	244
	inventory	J	284
	est. acct.	U	147
William	will (1701 - Stafford Co.)*		
William H.	will	Q	57
	inventory	Q	68
	inventory (Stafford Co.)	Q	70
	est. acct.	R	16
FLEMING			
Thomas	will	E	160
FLOOD			
Thomas	will	K	221
FLOYD			
Ebeneezer	admr. bond	A1 pt. 1	10
	inventory	A1 pt. 1	25
	est. acct.	A1 pt. 1	67

Name	Document	Will Book	Page
FLOYD (continued)			
John	admr. bond	A1 pt. 1	18
	inventory	A1 pt. 1	30
	est. acct.	A1 pt. 1	121
FOLLIN			
John	inventory	T	397
	sale acct.	U	186
	est. acct.	U	203, 205, 412, 413
	est. acct.	V	18
Mary Jane	see PEARSON, Mary Jane		
FOLLIN see also FALLEN			
FOOTE			
Stephen D.	gdn. acct.	U	430
	gdn. acct.	V	161
	gdn. bond	Sup. Ct.	101
William H.	will	V	5
	inventory	V	74, 227
	sale acct.	V	83
	est. acct.	V	243
	est. acct.	W	16
	exr. acct.	W	231
FORD			
Thomas	will	C	257
	inventory	D	7
FOREMAN			
Peter	will	I	408
FOSTER			
John	will	J	55

Name	Document	Will Book	Page
FOWLER			
John	inventory	J	122
	sale acct.	J	124
	est. acct.	J	295
	est. acct.	K	139
	est. acct.	P	164
Lucy	will	V	406
	inventory	W	61
FOX			
Albert	gdn. bond	V	11, 63, 330
Amos	will	I	516
	inventory	K	111
Amos	gdn. bond	V	23
	gdn. acct.	W	243
Ann	will	K	99
	inventory	L	175*
Eugenia	gdn. bond	V	10, 63, 330
Francis	gdn. bond	V	9
	gdn. acct.	W	245
Gabriel	inventory	U	263*
	sale acct.	U	358
	sale acct.	V	118
	est. acct.	V	171
	est. acct.	W	60, 277
George	gdn. bond	V	9, 62, 329
Isaac	inventory	L	192
	est. acct.	U	6
Margaret	will	R	128
	inventory	R	143
	sale acct.	R	334
	est. acct.	U	6
	est. acct.*		
Mary	gdn. bond	V	8
FRANCIS			
Henry	will	T	222
	sale acct.	T	304

Name	Document	Will Book	Page
FRAZIER			
William H.	inventory	V	338
FRENCH			
Daniel	will	A1 pt. 2	269b
	exor. bond	A1 pt. 2	269b
	inventory	A1 pt. 2	289
	est. acct.	B	102
Daniel	will	C	134
	inventory	C	168
	est. acct.	C	196
	est. acct.	D	34
FRIZZEL			
Luke	will	I	373
William	will	C	48
	inventory	C	52
FROBEL			
John J.	will	W	161*
	inventory	W	211
FRYER			
William	inventory	D	2
	admr. bond	Bond Bk.	130
FULLER			
Hiram	will	W	157*
	inventory	X	31*
	sale acct.	X	34
	est. acct.	X	137, 435
Robert	admr. bond	G	120
FULLMER			
John A.	will	P	248
	inventory	P	255

Name	Document	Will Book	Page
FURGUSON see FERGUSON			
GANTT			
John	inventory	T	133
	sale acct.	T	166
	est. acct.	U	691, 315*
	div. of slaves	U	319
Priscilla J.	gdn. bond	T	242
	gdn. acct.	U	23
William H.	committee bond	T	175
	committee bond	U	191
	committee acct.	V	275
	committee acct.	W	358
	committee acct.	X	412, 443
GARDENHIRE			
Jacob	inventory	B	420
	admr. bond	Bond Bk.	76
GARDNER			
Joseph	inventory	J	354
	est. acct.	L	158*
	heirs acct.	L	160
Mary	dower allotted	L	162*
Mary J.	will	K	109
	inventory	K	329
GARRARD			
Henry	inventory	T	327
	sale acct.	T	328
GARRETT			
Edward	inventory	A1 pt. 2	510
	est. acct.	B	68
Nicholas	will	G	84
	exor. bond	G	96

Name	Document	Will Book	Page

GARRETT (continued)
Obediah	est. acct.	K	367
	inventory	K	369
	sale acct.	K	371
William	will	D	81
	inventory	D	89

GARVEY
| Ann Ruth | gdn. bond | E | 255 |

GATES
| Samuel | admr. bond | G | 47 |

GERMAN see **JERMAN**

GIBNEY
| Hugh | inventory | E | 88 |

GIBSON
| Sybill | will | E | 19 |

GIDDENS see **GITTINGS**

GILHAM
| John | will | V | 297 |
| | inventory | V | 324 |

GILL
| Presley | gdn. bond | N | 85 |

GITTINGS
Thomas	admr. bond	A1 pt. 2	269a
	est. acct.	A1 pt. 2	273
	inventory	A1 pt. 2	273
	est. acct.	A1 pt. 2	401

GLADDING see **GLADIN**

Name	Document	Will Book	Page
GLADIN			
Ann	inventory	B	31
	admr. bond	Bond Bk.	4
	admr. acct.*		
Francis	will	B	180
	inventory	B	239
	est. acct.	B	240
John	will	A1 pt. 2	302
	exor. bond	A1 pt. 2	304, 305
	inventory	B	3
	admr. bond	Bond Bk.	80
GLOVER			
John W.	gdn. bond	R	201
Josiah	gdn. bond	R	201
Susanna E.	gdn. bond	R	201
GOARD			
Mary	will	D	1

GOARD see also GORD

GODDARD
    William   will (1814 - Alexandria - see FDB V2:344)

GODFREY			
William	will	B	13
	inventory	B	23

GOIN see GOWEN

GOLDUP			
John	will	K	325
	inventory	L	110*
	sale acct.	L	111

Name	Document	Will Book	Page
GOODING			
Elizabeth	will	N	148
Jacob	admr. bond	F	144
John	gdn. bond	E	101
John	will	L	58
	inventory	L	122*
William	gdn. bond	K	424
GOODS			
George	admr. bond	G	51
	sale acct.	G	266
GOODWIN			
Matthew	inventory	B	142
	admr. bond	Bond Bk.	39
GORD			
Joseph	admr. bond	Bond Bk.	137
GORD see also GOARD			
GORDON			
David	admr. bond	Bond Bk.	126
	inventory	C	191
	sale acct.	C	193
James	will	Sup. Ct.	111
	admr. bond	Sup. Ct.	112
	sale acct.	S	369
John	gdn. bond	T	296
Martha T.	inventory	S	359
	sale acct.	S	361
	est. acct.	U	107
William W.	gdn. bond	U	84
GOSSOM			
Alexander W.	will	N	210
	inventory	N	222
	sale acct.	N	225
	est. acct.	O	421

Name	Document	Will Book	Page
GOSSOM (continued)			
Fanny	est. acct.	T	144, 277
Thomas	will	Q	165
	inventory	R	214
	inventory	S	471
	sale acct.	S	475, 479
	est. acct.	T	144, 277
William	will	C	230
	inventory	C	235
GOWEN			
Daniel	admr. bond	G	104
	inventory	G	113, 192
Richard	will	L	179
	inventory	L	185
GOWIN see **GOWEN**			
GRACE			
Patrick	will	E	164
	inventory	E	200
	sale acct.	E	201
	est. acct.	E	202
GRADY			
Francis	admr. bond	A1 pt. 2	354
	inventory	A1 pt. 2	380
	est. acct.	B	30
GRAHAM			
Adeline	gdn. bond	V	307
Ann Matilda	see BRADLEY, Ann Matilda		
Edward	will	A1 pt. 2	327
	exor. bond	A1 pt. 2	328
	inventory	A1 pt. 2	445
Elizabeth Mary			
Ann Barnes	will	L	60

Name	Document	Will Book	Page
GRAHAM (continued)			
Hugh	inventory	W	169
	sale acct.	W	172
	est. acct.	W	365*
Robert	inventory	A1 pt. 2	529
	est. acct.	B	89
GRANT			
Nancy	gdn. bond	G	103
GRANTUM			
John	inventory	B	58
	est. acct.	B	59
	admr. bond	Bond Bk.	5
GRAY			
John	inventory	E	1
Spencer	will (1825 - Alexandria - see FDB V2:344)		
GRAYSON			
Benjamin	inventory	C	240, 25
	admr. bond	Bond Bk.	89
Sinah Elizabeth	gdn. bond	J	62
GREADY see **GRADY**			
GREEN			
Charles	will	B	298
Eve	sale acct.	R	222
	inventory	R	226
	est. acct.	S	349
James	inventory	B	339
	admr. bond	Bond Bk.	32
Thomas	admr. bond	G	135
	inventory	G	327
William	will (1692 - Bermuda)*		

Name	Document	Will Book	Page
GREENWAY			
Joseph	admr. bond	F	299
	inventory	G	90
GRETTER			
John, heirs	gdn. acct.	J	56
Margaret, heirs	gdn. acct.	J	56
Michael	gdn. bond	H	34
GRIFFIN			
Ezekiel	inventory	B	46
	est. acct.	B	53
	admr. bond	Bond Bk.	12
John	will	X	247
Walter	will	U	446
	est. acct.	V	357
GRIFFITH			
David	admr. bond	E	347
Elizabeth	gdn. bond	F	295
Margaret	gdn. acct.	J	55
Samuel G.	est. acct.	Q	200, 208
	est. acct.	U	213, 215
GRIMES			
Catharine	est. acct.	C	22
George	inventory	P	136
	sale acct.	P	137
	est. acct.	P	162
John	est. acct.	C	22
William	inventory	B	146, 183
	div. of est.	B	224, 229, 231
	gdn. acct.	B	366
	est. acct.	B	22
	admr. bond	Bond Bk.	35b
GRIMWOOD			
William	admr. bond	A1 pt. 1	193
	inventory	A1 pt. 1	202
	est. acct.	A1 pt. 1	206

Name	Document	Will Book	Page
GROVES			
John	admr. bond	G	174
	inventory	G	178
GULLATT			
John	will	E	5
Peter	inventory	E	81
GUMMERSON			
Elizabeth	admr. bond	A1 pt. 2	301
William	admr. bond	A1 pt. 1	1
	inventory	A1 pt. 1	23
GUNNELL			
Allen	inventory	Q	53
	sale acct.	Q	55
	est. acct.	R	22
	est. acct.	S	184, 357, 504
	est. acct.	T	194
Allen	gdn. bond	T	98
Ann	will	N	44
Catharine	est. acct.	O	335
Catharine V.	gdn. bond	W	155
Elizabeth	will (1827 - Frederick Co.)*		
	inventory of dower slaves	Q	109
Henry	will	F	58
	exor. bond	F	75
	est. acct.	I	422
Henry	will	M	301
	inventory	M	330
	sale acct.	N	163
	est. acct.	P	320
Henry Jr.	will	E	190
	inventory	E	345
James	will (1819 - Fauquier Co.)*		
Jemima	gdn. bond	S	353

Name	Document	Will Book	Page
GUNNELL (continued)			
John	will	H	133
	est. acct.	Q	157
Joshua C.	gdn. bond	M	387
	gdn. acct.	S	94
Nancy	inventory	M	383
	will	M	401
	inventory	P	178, 191
	est. acct.	P	308
Robert	will	L	176*
	est. acct.	O	337
Robert	will	P	173
Robert	will	W	86
Thomas	admr. bond	H	231
	admr. bond	I	52
	est. acct.	O	341
Thomas Jr.	sale acct.	N	379
William	will	B	218
	inventory	B	222
William	will	F	339
	exor. bond	G	188
	inventory	I	75
	sale acct.	I	79
	est. acct.	I	82
William	will	M	423
(son of Thomas)	sale acct.	N	253
	inventory	N	254
	est. acct.	N	347
	est. acct.	O	207
William, Dr.	will	R	201
	inventory	S	246
	sale acct.	S	252
	est. acct.	S	326, 529
	est. acct.	T	155
	est. acct.	U	217
	accts. due est.*		
	partial est. acct.*		

Name	Document	Will Book	Page
GUNNELL (continued)			
William	will	V	214
	inventory	V	407
	sale acct.	W	181
	division	W	296
William Jr.	est. acct.	P	326
GUNSTON			
John	inventory	B	162
	admr. bond	Bond Bk.	27
GUPTON			
William	inventory	B	132
	admr. bond	Bond Bk.	35a
GWINN see GWYNN			
GWYNN			
Benjamin	will	G	214
	exor. bond	G	216
	inventory	G	240
Hooper	inventory	B	203
	admr. bond	Bond Bk.	51
Humphrey	div. of slaves	K	82
HAISLIP			
Abigail	will	P	279
	inventory	P	331
	est. acct.	S	110
Andrew J.	gdn. bond	R	369
Ann	gdn. bond	Q	374
	gdn. acct.	T	267
Arthur L.	gdn. bond	R	342*
Harriet E.	gdn. bond	R	342*
Henry	will	Q	50
	est. acct.	T	44
	exor. bond	T	183

Name	Document	Will Book	Page
HAISLIP (continued)			
James	will	I	259
Silas	gdn. bond	Q	372
	gdn. acct.	T	267
HALBERT			
Michael	gdn. bond	I	309
Thomas	inventory	D	215
	admr. bond	Bond Bk.	171
HALE			
William	admr. bond	Bond Bk.	9
HALL			
Andrew J.	gdn. bond	S	393
	gdn. bond	U	401
Archibald	inventory	S	304
	sale acct.	S	397
	est. acct.	S	447
Casandra	will	Sup. Ct.	155
	curator's bond	Sup. Ct.	157
	inventory	Sup. Ct.	161
Daniel	gdn. bond	S	393
	gdn. bond	U	401
Dinah	gdn. bond	S	393
	gdn. bond	U	401
Elisha	will	A1 pt. 2	440
	inventory	A1 pt. 2	483
Elizabeth	admr. bond	G	94
Elizabeth	inventory	T	297
	sale acct.	T	299
	est. acct.	T	360
Futerall	inventory	B	419
	est. acct.	C	9
	admr. bond	Bond Bk.	79
Isaac	curator's bond	Sup. Ct.	157
James F.	inventory	X	310

Name	Document	Will Book	Page
HALL (continued)			
John	inventory	B	143
	est. acct.	B	187, 233
Keronhappuch	admr. bond	G	59
	inventory	G	85
	est. acct.	G	86
Mary	admr. bond	A1 pt. 2	322
Michael	will	E	266
	inventory	E	270
	est. acct.	G	81
Susan	est. acct.	X	366
William	inventory	A1 pt. 2	412
William Sr.	will	Q	281b
	inventory	R	76
	sale acct.	R	78
	div. of slaves	R	178
	est. acct.	R	309
HALLEY			
Catherine	will	J	74
	inventory	J	134
	est. acct.	N	349
	est. acct.	P	185
	est. acct. (see CFF#82v - Suddath's admrs vs. Halley's exr. - 1825)		
George	will	N	168
Henry S.	will	S	541
	exor. bond	S	542
	est. acct.	T	358
	inventory	U	284
	sale acct.	U	290*
	est. acct.	X	267
James Sr.	will	F	134
	exor. bond	F	139
	inventory	F	271
John H.	est. acct.	V	148
	est. acct.	W	9
	est. acct.	X	28

Name	Document	Will Book	Page
HALLEY (continued)			
Nathaniel	est. acct.	L	291
Samuel	will	D	117
	inventory	D	201
Samuel S.	inventory	U	399
	sale acct.	U	440
Sarah	inventory	W	349*
	sale acct.	X	7
	est. acct.	X	26*
William	will	I	460
	inventory	J	126
	inventory	L	372
	est. acct.	O	284
	est. acct.	P	185
	est. acct.	R	7
	div. of slaves (see FDB G2:380)		
	est. acct.(see CFF#82v - Suddath's admr. vs. Halley's exor. - 1825)		
William	will	Sup. Ct.	50
	admr. bond	Sup. Ct.	51
William	will	P	330
	est. acct.	R	50
	est. acct.	S	203
HALLING			
Benjamin	admr. bond	A1 pt. 1	145
	inventory	A1 pt. 1	154
	est. acct.	A1 pt. 1	204
John	will	A1 pt. 1	162
	exor. bond	A1 pt. 1	163
	inventory	A1 pt. 1	212
	est. acct.	B	47
Reubin	will	A1 pt. 1	138
	exor. bond	A1 pt. 1	139
	inventory	A1 pt. 1	156
William	will	A1 pt. 2	344
	inventory	A1 pt. 2	408

Name	Document	Will Book	Page
HAMILTON			
Eli	gdn. bond	U	382
Joseph	admr. bond	F	73
Samuel	will	U	380
HAMMERSLEY			
Elizabeth	inventory	L	50
Francis	inventory	J	385
HAMPTON			
Ann	gdn. bond	H	247
	gdn. acct.	J	276
Henry	gdn. bond	H	247
	gdn. acct.	I	276
James R.	gdn. bond	W	159
John	will	A1 pt. 1	264
	exor. bond	A1 pt. 1	265
	inventory	A1 pt. 2	309
John	admr. bond	G	14, 281
	inventory	G	75
	inventory	H	248
	est. acct.	I	414
	slaves sold	J	279
John	gdn. bond	H	247
	gdn. acct.	I	276
Laura V.	gdn. bond	W	159
Lucy E.	gdn. bond	W	159
Margaret	inventory	C	156
	est. acct.	C	157
	admr. bond	Bond Bk.	100
Mary	gdn. bond	K	138
	gdn. bond	M	325
	gdn. acct.	O	247
Sarah Elizabeth	gdn. bond	H	247
Sinah	gdn. bond	H	247
	gdn. acct.	I	276

Name	Document	Will Book	Page

HAMPTON (continued)

William	will	M	75
	inventory	M	370
	est. acct.	O	19
William H.	gdn. bond	W	159
	gdn. acct.	Z	264*

HANCOCK

George	will	I	385
	est. acct.	J	236
William	gdn. bond	H	177

HANNAH

Nicholas	admr. bond	G	39

HARDEN

Ann	gdn. bond	D	259
Charles	gdn. bond	D	259
Daniel	gdn. bond	D	259
Nancy	will	K	138
Thomas G.	gdn. bond	D	306
William	gdn. bond	D	259
William	will	D	236
	inventory	D	237, 239
	division	D	334

HARDEN see also HARDING

HARDING

George	inventory	K	175
	est. acct.	M	89
William	will	S	25
	inventory	S	67

HARDING see also HARDEN

Name	Document	Will Book	Page
HARLE			
John	admr. bond	A1 pt. 2	298
	will	A1 pt. 2	300
	inventory	A1 pt. 2	340
	inventory	B	47
	sale acct.	B	268b
	est. acct.	B	291
	est. acct.	D	84
Sarah	inventory	E	19
William	will	A1 pt. 2	332
	exor. bond	A1 pt. 2	335
	est. acct.	A1 pt. 2	536
	inventory	A1 pt. 2	537
	sale acct.	B	270
	est. acct.	B	294
	est. acct.	D	84
HARLEY			
William	inventory	M	338
	est. acct.	N	203
HARMAN			
Elizabeth	will	X	69
Peter	will	K	77
	est. acct.	L	120*
HARPER			
Ann	gdn. bond	I	403
John Withers	inventory	A1 pt. 2	475
Mary	gdn. bond	K	138
Nancy	admr. bond	K	138
Robert	will	D	262
	inventory	D	264
	admr. bond	E	322
	est. acct.	G	295

HARPERWITHERS
John   see HARPER, John Withers

Name	Document	Will Book	Page
HARRINGTON			
Henry	est. acct.	A1 pt. 2	288
Lucy	est. acct.	V	249
	est. acct.	X	346
HARRIS			
Anthony	inventory	D	56
	admr. bond	Bond Bk.	155
Benjamin	will	F	192
	exor. bond	F	195, 233
	inventory	G	343
	est. acct.	G	348
	sale acct.	I	529
Elizabeth	will	K	409
Hezekiah	gdn. bond	F	297
Hezekiah	inventory	K	407
	sale acct.	K	408
	est. acct.	K	411
	est. acct.	O	318
John	admr. bond	A1 pt. 1	254
Sarah Ann	will	J	394
	see also BROADWATER, Sarah Ann		
William G.	gdn. bond	O	57
HARRISON			
Catherine	gdn. bond	N	46
George	will	A1 pt. 1	260
	exor. bond	A1 pt. 1	261
	inventory	A1 pt. 2	279, 531
	est. acct.	A1 pt. 2	532
Jeremiah	will	A1 pt. 2	384
	exor. bond	A1 pt. 2	397
	inventory	A1 pt. 2	425
John D.	will (1853 - Alexandria)*		
Thomas	inventory	B	154, 165
Thomas Jr.	admr. bond	Bond Bk.	29

Name	Document	Will Book	Page
HARRISON (continued)			
William	inventory	N	122
	sale acct.	N	127
	est. acct.	O	278
HARRISS see HARRIS			
HARROVER			
Sinah	inventory	Q	172
	sale acct.	Q	174
	est. acct.	R	251
HART			
Joseph	inventory	X	188
	sale acct.	X	191
	est. acct.	X	434
HARTLEY			
James	inventory	H	29
HARTSHORNE			
William	will	1	202
HARWOOD			
Mary E.	gdn. bond	O	366
	gdn. bond	P	282
	gdn. acct.	P	337
Matilda G.	gdn. bond	O	366
	gdn. bond (2)	P	92
HATTERSLEY			
William	admr. bond	G	122
HAWKINS			
John	inventory	B	72
Mary	will	D	8
	inventory	D	22
	est. acct.	D	64

Name	Document	Will Book	Page

HAWLEY see HALLEY

HAWTHORNE
| Hannah | will | E | 187* |

HAYCOCK
| John | inventory | W | 297 |

HEALEY
Mary	will	E	356
	exor. bond	E	358
	inventory	I	199
	sale acct.	I	205
	est. acct.	I	209

HEARD
John	admr. bond	G	98
	inventory	G	120
	est. acct.	G	242

HEATON
John	inventory	D	307
	sale acct.	D	312
	est. acct.	D	355
	est. acct.	G	231
	admr. bond	Bond Bk.	136

HEDGES
Elmira	gdn. bond	U	439
Fairfax	gdn. bond	U	439
Henry	inventory	U	439
Henry	gdn. bond	U	439
Sarah Ann	gdn. bond	U	439

HEINAMAN
| Jacob | will | M | 171 |
| | inventory | M | 405 |

Name	Document	Will Book	Page

HEINAMAN (continued)

Jacob (cont'd)	est. acct.	M	407
	est. acct.	N	207
	est. acct.	O	6

HELM

Charlotte F. (nee Ratcliffe)	gdn. acct.	P	269

HEMMERSLEY see HAMMERSLEY

HENDERSON

Ann	gdn. bond	R	331
Charles	inventory	M	259
	sale acct.	M	262
Charles W.	est. acct.	N	230
James	gdn. bond	R	331
	inventory	U	39
Robert W.	div. of slaves	R	328

HENINGER

Frederick	inventory	D	350

HENNING

John	inventory	R	127
	sale acct.	R	176
	est. acct.	R	253, 285
	est. acct.	S	450

HENSHAW

John	admr. bond	A1 pt. 2	336
	inventory	A1 pt. 2	385
	est. acct.	A1 pt. 2	488

HENSON

John	will	L	83*

Name	Document	Will Book	Page
HEPBURN			
William	will (1817 - Alexandria)		
HERBERT			
William	committee acct.	T	401
HEREFORD			
James	will	I	187
Jane (Jean)	will	B	52
	inventory	B	53

HEREFORD see also HERYFORD

HERIFORD see HEREFORD, HERYFORD

HERYFORD			
James	admr. bond	A1 pt. 1	59
	will	A1 pt. 1	60*
	inventory	A1 pt. 1	69
John	will	A1 pt. 1	44
	exor. bond	A1 pt. 1	46
	inventory	A1 pt. 1	56
	est. acct.	A1 pt. 1	153

HERYFORD see also HEREFORD

HESS			
Jacob	will	E	251
HEWITT			
Thomas W.	will	R	244
HEWS			
Charles	sale acct.	J	149

HEWS see also HUGHS

Name	Document	Will Book	Page
HICKSON see HIXSON			
HIGGS			
Benjamin F.	inventory	S	233
	sale acct.	S	238
	est. acct.	S	515
	est. acct.	U	297, 298
Benjamin F.	gdn. bond	U	200
	gdn. acct.	V	20
Charles F.	est. acct.	W	17
	gen. acct.	W	19
Julia F.	gdn. acct.	V	20
Thomas W.	gdn. acct.	V	20
HINDS			
Mathew	admr. bond	A1 pt. 2	348
	est. acct.	A1 pt. 2	422
	inventory	A1 pt. 2	422
HIPKINS			
Ann	gdn. bond	I	186
Elizabeth	gdn. bond	I	186
Lewis	will	G	34
	exor. bond	G	37
	inventory	H	163
	sale acct.	I	115
	est. acct.	I	121
Sarah	gdn. bond	I	186
Susannah	renounces provisions of husband		
	Lewis' will	G	97
HIXSON			
Elizabeth	will	N	132
HOFFMAN			
John T.	gdn. bond	R	368
	gdn. acct.	S	500

Name	Document	Will Book	Page
HOLLINGSHEAD			
John	inventory	C	113
	sale acct.	C	113
	est. acct.	C	114
	admr. bond	Bond Bk.	104
HOLLIS			
John	inventory	C	29
	est. acct.	C	42
	sale acct.	C	43
	admr. bond	Bond Bk.	92
HOOE			
Elizabeth Thompson	gdn. bond	T	394
James H.	will	N	339
	inventory	O	7
Joseph Thompson	gdn. bond	T	394
William F.	gdn. bond	M	334
	gdn. bond	N	167
	gdn. acct.*		
HOPPER			
James	will	H	161
Mary	will	I	46
HOPWOOD			
Moses	will	J	351
	inventory	K	6
	sale acct.	K	8
	est. acct.	O	285
HOUGH			
Lawrence	will	D	154
William	inventory	X	252
	sale acct.	X	253

Name	Document	Will Book	Page
HOWARD			
John Beal	will(1835 - Baltimore, Md.)*		
Samuel	will (1860)*		
HUBBALL			
Charles W. M.	gdn. bond	S	90
William	sale acct.	S	365
	est. acct.*		
HUDSON			
John	admr. bond	A1 pt. 2	400
	inventory	A1 pt. 2	423
	est. acct.	A1 pt. 2	508
Sarah	gdn. bond	K	38
HUGHLEY see HUGULEY			
HUGHS			
John	inventory	X	255
	sale acct.	X	259
HUGHS see also HEWS			
HUGULEY			
George	inventory	J	427
	est. acct.	M	205
	inventory	Sup. Ct.	25
Jacob	inventory	J	380
	sale acct.	J	382
	est. acct.	J	383
Job	will	J	377
HULL			
John	admr. bond	Bond Bk.	618
HULLS			
George	exor. bond	Sup. Ct.	159
	will	Sup. Ct.	160

Name	Document	Will Book	Page
HUME			
Robert	sale acct.	T	142
	est. acct.	U	3
HUMPHREYS			
Samuel	inventory	F	151
	will	F	320
	exor. bond	F	321
HUNT see HUNTT			
HUNTER			
Catherine	gdn. bond	G	381
	inventory	P	146
George	will	C	257
George	inventory	H	95
	est. acct.	I	232
	est. acct.	J	88
	admr. bond	K	53
	est. acct.	K	53
	est. acct.	M	322
	est. acct.	O	415
Hannah	gdn. bond	G	381
Jane Naomi	gdn. bond	G	381
John	will	B	364
	inventory	B	404, 411
John	will	K	266*
	inventory	L	167*
	sale acct.	M	40
	est. acct.	O	253
William Jr.	will	F	202
HUNTINGTON			
John	inventory	V	34
	sale acct.	W	136
	est. acct.	W	144

Name	Document	Will Book	Page
HUNTT			
George W.	gdn. bond	S	73, 273
	gdn. acct.	U	423
Gerrard	will	S	219
	curator's bond	S	228
	est. acct.	U	1
Gerrard L. W.	inventory	S	99
	sale acct.	S	100
	est. acct.	S	438
	est. acct.	U	192
James	will	M	128
	inventory	T	106
	est. acct.	U	120
Orlando W.	gdn. bond	S	73, 273
	gdn. acct.	U	426
Susan C.	gdn. bond	S	73, 273
	gdn. acct.	U	424
HURST			
Daniel	will	U	181
James	inventory	B	420
	est. acct.	B	421
	admr. bond	Bond Bk.	828*
John	exr. bond	E	348
	will	E	349
	inventory	F	28, 34
	est. acct.	G	370
William	gdn. bond	E	405
HUSKINS			
William	will	I	390
	inventory	I	504
	sale acct.	J	139
	est. acct.	J	143

HUTCHINSON see HUTCHISON

Name	Document	Will Book	Page
HUTCHISON			
Benjamin	will	N	174
	inventory	O	23
	sale acct.	P	405
	sale acct.	R	323
	est. acct.	S	125
	est. acct.	S	437
	distribution acct.	S	507
Elijah	will	V	4
	inventory	V	59
	sale acct.	V	199, 299
Elizabeth	will	R	131
	inventory	R	231
	sale acct.	R	233
	est. acct.	S	128, 313
Harriet	gdn. bond	L	82
Jeremiah	inventory	P	388
	will (1823 - unprobated)*		
	sale acct.	P	390
	est. acct.	Q	123
	est. acct.	R	103, 351
	est. acct.	S	523
John	will	H	90
	inventory	H	148
	est. acct.	I	8
Joshua	will	U	38
	inventory	U	266*
	sale acct.	U	269*
	est. acct.	U	302*
	exor. bond	V	176
	est. acct.	V	401
	est. acct.	X	152, 233
Lewis	inventory	X	396
	sale acct.	X	397
Martha	inventory	P	250

Name	Document	Will Book	Page
HUTCHISON (continued)			
Mary Ann	settlement with Jeremiah		
	Hutchison's admr.	R	351
	will	U	276
	est. acct.	U	277
	inventory	U	278*
	sale acct.	V	57
	est. acct.	X	352, 447
Samuel	will	K	269
	inventory	K	351
	sale acct.	N	196
	est. acct.	O	331
JACKSON			
Charles W.	gdn. bond	T	1
David	inventory	E	361
George Wm.			
Washington	gdn. bond	Q	111
	gdn. bond	R	147
	gdn. acct.	S	114, 490
Harriet L.	gdn. bond	P	424
James W.	gdn. bond	U	98
John	will	E	87
	inventory	E	100
John Sr.	will	L	319
	est. acct.	O	288
	est. acct.	R	112
	inventory	R	391
	sale acct.	S	18
	est. acct.	S	123, 491
John T. J.	gdn. bond	Q	110
	gdn. bond	R	147
	gdn. acct.	S	111, 488
	will	W	158*
Penelope	nuncupative will	S	267
	sale acct.	S	467

Name	Document	Will Book	Page

JACKSON (continued)

Richard	will	N	206
	est. acct.	P	194
	exor. acct.	P	197
	est. acct.	Q	155
	inventory	S	1
	est. acct.	S	130
Robert	inventory	K	359, 360
Spencer	inventory	Q	168*
	est. acct.	Q	369
	est. acct.	R	339
	est. acct. (see CFF#52e - Jackson vs. Jackson - 1835)		
	sale acct.	S	458
Spencer	gdn. bond*		

JACOBS

Alfred	gdn. bond	R	379
	gdn. acct.	T	185
Benjamin	inventory	J	422
	est. acct.	K	67
	est. acct.	L	81, 371
	est. acct.	Q	220
Elizabeth (Betsy)	curator's bond	W	179
	will	W	180
	div. of slaves	W	213
Harrison	gdn. bond	R	379
	gdn. acct.	T	185*
Joseph	will	K	265
Sarah	gdn. bond	H	247
Zebret	gdn. bond	E	197

JANNEY

Amos	admr. bond	A1 pt. 1	206
John	will	N	145
	inventory	N	268b

Name	Document	Will Book	Page

JANNEY (continued)

Jonathan	will	T	8
	exor. bond	T	9
	est. acct.	U	155

JAVAIN see **JAVINS**

JAVINS

Edgar S.	gdn. bond	U	362
	gdn. acct.	X	149
Jean	gdn. bond	G	100
Jefferson	gdn. bond	G	100
John	inventory	L	7
Joseph	inventory	B	235
	est. acct.	B	330
	admr. bond	Bond Bk.	57
Mary	gdn. bond	G	100
Sebastian	gdn. bond	G	100

JENKINS

Anna	est. acct.	R	282
Benjamin	children gdn. bond	R	200
Charles	inventory	J	358
Cynthia L.	gdn. bond	K	401
Elisha	gdn. bond	Q	82, 246
Elisha	inventory	Q	178b
	sale acct.	Q	185
	est. acct.	Q	286
	children gdn. bond	R	81
	est. acct.	S	187
Ezekiel	exor. bond	A1 pt. 2	395
	will	A1 pt. 2	404
	inventory	A1 pt. 2	414, 466, 510
	est. acct.	B	92
Elenor	will (see C.O.B.1807:192)		

Name	Document	Will Book	Page
JENKINS (continued)			
Fanny	gdn. bond	R	200
	gdn. bond	U	11
James	gdn. bond	R	81
	gdn. acct.	S	127
James Sr.	est. acct.	G	32
James W.	gdn. bond	Q	126
	gdn. bond	U	174
	gdn. acct.	V	349
	gdn. acct.	W	113
John	inventory	A1 pt. 2	528
	est. acct.	B	35
John L.	gdn. bond	M	311
Lozetta	gdn. bond	R	200
Margaret	nuncupative will	I	155, 386
	inventory	J	3
	sale acct.	J	5
	inventory	L	364
	sale acct.	M	242
	est. acct.	M	242
	est. acct.	N	358
Priscilla	will	J	388
	inventory	J	397
	est. acct.	K	333
Priscilla	gdn. bond	Q	126
	gdn. bond	R	81
	gdn. acct.	S	127
Rufus	gdn. bond	R	200
	gdn. acct.	V	18
Samuel	will	E	392
	exor. bond	E	395
	inventory	F	9
Samuel	inventory	L	367
	sale acct.	M	242
	est. acct.	M	242
	est. acct. (1826)*		

Name	Document	Will Book	Page
JENKINS (continued)			
Simon	will	F	186
	exor. bond	F	187, 209
	inventory	F	239
	inventory	J	99
	sale acct.	J	100
	est. acct.	J	101
Susan	gdn. acct.	Q	52
	gdn. bond	R	200
	gdn. acct.	V	18
Thomas	gdn. bond	R	200
	gdn. acct.	V	18
Thomas	admr. bond	A1 pt. 1	114
	inventory	A1 pt. 1	117
William	exor. bond	A1 pt. 1	209
	will	A1 pt. 1	210
	inventory	A1 pt. 1	229
William	will	V	228
Zachariah	admr. bond	Bond Bk.	162
JENNINGS			
Alexander	will	A1 pt. 2	469
	inventory	A1 pt. 2	493
Daniel	will	B	72
	inventory	B	109
	est. acct.	B	133
	sale acct.	C	6
JERMAN			
Nancy	gdn. bond	M	170
JETT			
Catherine	gdn. bond	O	209
JEWELL			
Smallwood R.	inventory	U	238
	sale acct.	U	239

Name	Document	Will Book	Page
JOACHIM			
Henry	inventory	K	298
JOHNSON			
Mildred	gdn. bond	M	333
Samuel	will	C	177
	inventory	C	189
Thornton	will	X	171
	inventory	X	250
William	will	J	227

JOHNSON see also JOHNSTON

Name	Document	Will Book	Page
JOHNSTON			
Bennett	will	L	337
Daniel	gdn. bond	R	175
Dennis	inventory	W	299
	admr. bond	Sup. Ct.	152
Francis	gdn. bond	K	327
French	gdn. bond	R	175
George	will	B	432
	est. acct.	B	439
	inventory	C	1
George	gdn. bond	R	175
Hannah	will	C	123
	inventory	C	132
Margaret	gdn. bond	R	175
Mary	will	C	73
	inventory	C	99, 229
Polly	gdn. bond	R	175
Samuel	will	C	53

JOHNSTON see also JOHNSON

Name	Document	Will Book	Page
JONES			
Ann	will	U	46

Name	Document	Will Book	Page
JONES (continued)			
Charles	will	G	303
	exor. bond	G	304
	inventory	G	308
David	admr. bond	A1 pt. 1	214
	inventory	A1 pt. 1	218
	sale acct.	A1 pt. 1	218
	est. acct.	A1 pt. 1	223
Deborah	will	L	208
Elizabeth Lee	will	N	49*
Emily	gdn. bond	Sup. Ct.	120
John	inventory	A1 pt. 2	474
	est. acct.	A1 pt. 2	475
John	will	I	139
Lettice Corbin	will (1804 - Northumberland Co.)*		
Lewin	will	K	307
	inventory	Q	419
	est. acct.	S	156
Notley	inventory	I	395
Robert	inventory	C	63
	admr. bond	Bond Bk.	95
Roger	inventory	X	15*
	sale acct.	X	17
Sarah Ann	will	P	28
Sarah Ann	gdn. bond	V	73
KEENE			
James	will	B	301
	inventory	B	305, 339
	division	B	349
	est. acct.	B	377
James Jr.	div. of slaves	R	148
	inventory	R	149
	acct. of slaves	R	179
	will	R	375
	inventory	S	39
	sale acct.	S	41

Name	Document	Will Book	Page
KEENE (continued)			
James Jr. (cont'd)	est. acct.	S	160
	est. acct.	T	403
Matilda	gdn. bond	N	293
William	will	J	41
William	will	V	320
	inventory	W	121
	sale acct.	W	124
	est. acct.	Sup. Ct.	158
KEITH			
James	will	N	294
	inventory		
	(Fairfax Co.)	O	122
	(Alexandria)	O	127
	(Berkeley Co.)	O	129
	est. acct.	O	186
	est. acct.	P	156
	est. acct.	Q	61, 289
James Sr.	est. acct.	R	314
William	est. acct.	Q	148
KELLER			
Michael	will	L	63
KELLY			
James	inventory	D	245
	sale acct.	D	245
	admr. bond	Bond Bk.	178
KENNEDY			
Eliza	will	X	70
	inventory	X	175

KENNEDY see also CANADY

Name	Document	Will Book	Page
KENT			
Benoni	will	C	194
	inventory	C	212
Richard	will	B	213
	inventory	B	228
Richard	will	C	117
	inventory	C	139
	admr. bond	Bond Bk.	110
KERBY see KIRBY			
KIDWELL			
Alexander	will	K	287
	inventory	K	308
	sale acct.	K	331
	est. acct.	M	291
Hezekiah	inventory	H	191
	sale acct	H	244
	est. acct.	H	245
James	will	X	371
Jane Eliza.	gdn. bond	O	121
Mary	inventory	L	63
Mary	gdn. bond	P	1
KINCHELOE			
Daniel	will	E	115
	inventory	E	133
Hector Sr.	will	V	362
	inventory	V	403
	sale acct.	V	405
	inventory	W	90
	sale acct.	W	90
Nestor	will	H	184
	admr. bond	H	186
William	inventory	U	326*

Name	Document	Will Book	Page
KING			
Benjamin	will (1795 - Loudoun Co.)		
Hargess	will	N	42
	inventory	O	171
	sale acct.	O	174
	est. acct.	R	123
	est. acct.	S	339
James	inventory	C	38
	sale acct.	C	39
	est. acct.	C	88
	admr. bond	Bond Bk.	78
John	inventory	A1 pt. 2	500
	est. acct.	A1 pt. 2	500
	est. acct.	B	40
Samuel	admr. bond	A1 pt. 2	393
	inventory	A1 pt. 2	426
	est. acct.	A1 pt. 2	427
Winifred	will	N	296
	est. acct.	O	417
	acct. of slaves	R	221
KIPPS			
Eliza A.	see MITCHELL, Eliza A.		
KIRBY			
Ann Boggess	will	N	379
Ann (Nancy)	est. acct.	R	52
Robert B.	est. acct.	U	167
Thomas	will	I	279
	inventory	I	347
KIRK			
Robert William	gdn. bond	E	163
KIRKLAND			
Richard	will	A1 pt. 1	19
	exor. bond	A1 pt. 1	20
	inventory	A1 pt. 1	31

Name	Document	Will Book	Page
KIRKPATRICK			
Thomas	will	E	36
KITCHEN			
Daniel	will	S	387
	inventory	S	454
James	inventory	W	214
	sale acct.	W	216
	est. acct.	W	240
KITSON			
Samuel T.	gdn. bond	T	351
KNIGHT			
Angeline H.	will	R	148
Horatio	will	T	120
	inventory	T	138
	sale acct.	T	140
	est. acct.	U	236
LADD			
John G.	will	L	382
LAKE			
Jane	see LEGG, Jane		
Richard	will	C	225
LAKENAN			
Thomas D.	gdn. bond	R	88
LAMKIN			
George C.	will	K	242
	inventory	K	274
	est. acct.	L	180
LAMPHIER			
Venus	will	C	68
	inventory	C	79

Name	Document	Will Book	Page
LANCASTER			
Nathaniel	admr. bond	Bond Bk.	128
LANDMAN			
George	admr. bond	Bond Bk.	63
LANE			
Benedict M.	will	R	243
Catherine	will	Q	242
Charles	will	U	142
	inventory	U	143
	sale acct.	U	337
David	inventory	K	353
	sale acct.	K	355
	est. acct.	L	130*
	est. acct.	P	50
Elizabeth F.	will	S	104
Enoch S.	will	I	383
Francis W.	gdn. acct.	U	308*
Hardage	inventory	I	337, 444
Hardage	gdn. bond	I	334
Helen E.	gdn. bond	U	378
James W.	gdn. bond	U	378
Lydia	will	Sup. Ct.	75
	est. acct.	R	162
Philo R.	will	I	402
	inventory	K	202
	sale acct.	K	204
	est. acct. exceptions*		
Presley Carr	will	M	178
Richard	will	L	173*
	sale acct.	N	339
	est. acct.	O	265
	est. acct.	Q	37
Sarah	inventory	O	378
	est. acct.	R	83, 412
	est. acct.	S	108

Name	Document	Will Book	Page
LANE (continued)			
Susan	will	K	23
Susanna	will	Q	281
William	will	J	110
	inventory	J	224
	est. acct.	J	315
William	will	N	30
	inventory	N	169
	est. acct.	O	219, 344
	est. acct.	P	259, 266
	est. acct.	R	137
William Carr	will (Loudoun Co. - see FDB R2:320)		
William Hardage	gdn. bond	I	372
LANGMARCH			
Christian	will	D	413
LANHAM			
Edward	will	P	81
Electius	inventory	N	264
	sale acct.	N	267a
	est. acct.	O	407
	est. acct.	R	102
LASSWELL			
John	admr. bond	A1 pt. 1	146
	inventory	A1 pt. 1	157
LATIMER			
William	inventory	R	89
	est. acct.	R	257
	est. acct.	S	148
LAW			
Elizabeth P.	gdn. acct.	I	285
	gdn. acct.	K	123
Thomas	gdn. acct.	I	285

Name	Document	Will Book	Page
LAWRIE			
James	admr. bond	Bond Bk.	102
LAWSON			
Robert	will	G	435
	inventory	H	35
LAY			
Jemima	will	L	95
	inventory	M	207
	sale acct.	M	209
	est. acct.	N	355
Joseph	will	L	318
Joseph	will	Sup. Ct.	42
Sarah	will	G	421
	inventory	I	25

LAY see also LEIGH, LEE

LEAKE			
Richard	see LAKE, Richard		
LEE			
Ann H.	will	P	277
Francis L.	committee bond	M	51
	sale acct.	O	430
	inventory	P	13, 15
	debts	P	85
	committee acct.	P	149
	committee bond	Q	42
	inventory	Q	85
	committee acct.	Q	153
	committee resigns	R	411
	committee bond	R	411
	committee acct.	U	17, 31, 419
	committee accts.*		

Name	Document	Will Book	Page
LEE (continued)			
George W.	gdn. bond	V	1
John F.	admr. bond	Sup. Ct.	136, 138, 150
Philip D. C.	gdn. bond	V	2
Sinah E.	will	W	151
Thomas W.	inventory	U	24
	sale acct.	U	26
	div. of slaves	U	35
	est. acct.	U	178, 223
	est. acct.	V	198
William L.	inventory	R	317

LEE see also LEIGH, LAY

LEGG			
George	will	V	223
Jane	will	V	64
LEIGH			
Alfred	gdn. bond	Q	106
Cassius	gdn. bond	Q	106
	gdn. bond	S	274
Marmaduke C.	admr. bond	N	314
	inventory	N	325
	sale acct.	N	327
	est. acct.	O	93
	est. acct.	P	301
	div. of slaves	Q	391
	est. acct.	R	27, 46
Mary	gdn. bond	O	110
Matilda	gdn. bond	O	109
Samuel	gdn. bond	Q	106

LEIGH see also LAY, LEE

Name	Document	Will Book	Page
LEMOINE			
Francis E.	gdn. bond	S	470
Moreau	inventory	T	89
	est. acct.	T	143
LESLIE			
George	will	I	535
	inventory	J	95
LESTER			
William	will	C	241
	inventory	D	21
	est. acct.	D	68
LEWIS			
Catherine	gdn. bond	J	73
Daniel	inventory	M	172
	widow's dower	M	177
	sale acct.	N	322
	est. acct.	O	294
Eleanor P.	gdn. acct.	I	286, 299
	gdn. acct.	K	127
Eliza E.	gdn. bond	U	130
Elizabeth	dower	B	215
Elizabeth	will	T	332
Lawrence	will	T	127
Levi	will	R	245
Lucinda	gdn. bond	J	73
Lucy E.	gdn. bond	U	130
Stephen	inventory	B	157
	admr. bond	Bond Bk.	41
Susannah	gdn. bond	H	24
Thomas	will	A1 pt. 2	291
	exor. bond	A1 pt. 2	293
	inventory	A1 pt. 2	367
	est. acct.	B	64

Name	Document	Will Book	Page
LEWIS (continued)			
Thomas	will	C	124
	inventory	C	127
Thomas	est. acct.	V	246
William	admr. bond	G	61
	inventory	G	101
	est. acct.	G	429
William	gdn. bond	H	24
LIGHTFOOT			
Elizabeth	gdn. bond	S	272
Jane	gdn. bond	S	272
Mary Ann	gdn. bond	S	272
William	inventory	O	403, 404
	sale acct.	O	405
	est. acct.	P	160
LINDSAY			
Alfred	gdn. bond	K	362
Fanny	inventory	V	373
	sale acct.	W	2
	est. acct.	W	118
John	will	V	328
	inventory	V	375
	sale acct.	W	1
	est. acct.	W	230
Opie	will	K	250
	inventory	K	318
	div. of slaves	M	197
Robert	will	E	29
	inventory	H	156
	est. acct.	H	158
Sally	gdn. bond	K	362
Samuel	gdn. bond	K	362
Thomas	gdn. bond	K	76
Thomas	will	Q	125
	inventory	Q	246

Name	Document	Will Book	Page
LINDSAY (continued)			
Thomas (cont'd)	sale acct.	Q	350
	est. acct.	R	116
	est. acct.	S	139
William	admr. bond	F	313
	inventory	G	3
William	inventory	S	58
(son of Barnaby)	sale acct.	S	61
	est. acct.	S	177
William	inventory	U	434
	sale acct.	U	435
LINES			
Timothy	inventory	C	45
LINTON			
Moses	inventory	B	28
	admr. bond	Bond Bk.	1
William	inventory	C	99
	admr. bond	Bond Bk.	106
LITTLE			
Charles	inventory	J	423
	sale acct.	K	12
	est. acct.	L	26
LITTLETON			
John	will	A1 pt. 1	164
	exor. bond	A1 pt. 1	165
	inventory	A1 pt. 1	171
	est. acct.	A1 pt. 1	237
Lawson	will	X	5
LLOYD see **LOYD**			
LOGAN			
Thomas	admr. bond	Bond Bk.	143

Name	Document	Will Book	Page
LOMAX			
John	will	E	191
	est. acct.	F	13
LONG			
John Adam	admr. bond	Bond Bk.	49
LONGMARCH see **LANGMARCH**			
LOOMIS			
Josiah	will	X	14*
LOVE			
Frances Mildred	gdn. bond	L	211
John S.	inventory	P	244
	sale acct.	P	247
	est. acct.	Q	209
	sale acct.	Q	381
	est. acct.	R	56
	est. acct.	U	169
Samuel	will	H	173
	inventory	J	12
	sale acct.	J	14
	est. acct.	J	18
Thomas	will	F	251
LOVEJOY			
Margaret	will	Sup. Ct.	103
	admr. bond	Sup. Ct.	119
LOWE			
John	inventory	C	115
	admr. bond	Bond Bk.	108
LOWRY			
Ann	will (1834 - Fauquier Co.)		

Name	Document	Will Book	Page
LOYD			
Peter	will	B	329
	inventory	B	340
	est. acct.	B	367
LUCAS			
Jacob	admr. bond	A1 pt. 1	227
	inventory	A1 pt. 1	234, 267
	est. acct.	A1 pt. 2	297
Thomas	will	G	106
	est. acct.	M	13
LUMLEY			
John	admr. bond	Bond Bk.	50
LUNTT			
Ezra	inventory	U	85
LUPTON			
David	will	K	335
	est. acct.	N	143
LUTZ			
Michael	admr. bond	G	138
LYLE(S)			
Ann (Nancy) Eleanor			
	gdn. bond	E	189, 412
Robert Sr.	will	E	258
	inventory	E	263
William	will	L	197
LYNN			
Adam	will	E	144
	est. acct.	H	195

Name	Document	Will Book	Page
LYONS			
Timothy	admr. bond	Bond Bk.	94
MacDONALD see McDONALD			
MADDEN			
Hannah	will	G	431
MADDY			
William	est. acct.	B	106
	admr. bond	Bond Bk.	19
MAFFITT			
Sally	inventory	W	219
	est. acct.	W	239
William	inventory	Q	271
	est. acct.	Q	331
	est. acct.*		
MAGRUDER			
Ann	will	U	436
Greenberry	gdn. bond	O	165
Thomas	inventory	E	122
	est. acct.	G	185
	sale acct.	G	229
MAHONEY			
John	est. acct.	N	83
MANKIN			
Josias	inventory	B	423
	est. acct.	C	31
	admr. bond	Bond Bk.	77
MANLEY			
Harrison	will	C	215
	est. acct.	D	409
	est. acct.	G	6

Name	Document	Will Book	Page
MANLEY (continued)			
John	admr. bond	A1 pt. 2	351
	inventory	A1 pt. 2	383
	will	A1 pt. 2	469
	est. acct.	B	66
MANNING			
Deborah	will	U	241
John	will	A1 pt. 2	442
	inventory	B	11
MARSHALL			
George Francis	gdn. bond	W	159
	inventory	X	375
	est. acct.	X	439
James	will	Sup. Ct.	26
	exor. bond	Sup. Ct.	27
	inventory	Sup. Ct.	29
	sale acct.	Sup. Ct.	32
John	inventory	M	359
	sale acct.	M	362
	est. acct.	P	182
Richard	inventory	L	138*
	sale acct.	L	139
	est. acct.	L	140
Sarah	est. acct.	P	182
Susan Jane	gdn. bond	W	160
Simpson F.	gdn. bond	W	160
MARTIN			
George	inventory	C	191
	admr. bond	Bond Bk.	121
Jacob	inventory	T	116
	sale acct.	T	119
James	will	L	338

Name	Document	Will Book	Page
MARTIN (continued)			
John	will	B	131
	inventory	B	161
	admr. bond.	Bond Bk.	90
Nicholas	inventory	B	202
	admr. bond	Bond Bk.	52
MASON			
Ann	will	B	299
Charles	will	B	134
Edgar E.	gdn. bond	S	50
Ethelbert T.	gdn. bond	S	50
Francis	orphan's acct.	D	223
French	exor. bond	A1 pt. 1	255
	will	A1 pt. 1	256
	inventory	A1 pt. 2	287, 288
	est. acct.	A1 pt. 2	467
	inventory	C	26
	est. acct.	C	74
	admr. bond	Bond Bk.	88
George Sr.	will (1715)	PLC #2	13
George (of Gunston)	will	F	95
	exor. bond	F	182
George (of Lexington)	will	G	254a
	codicil	G	259
	exor. bond	G	261
	inventory	H	38
George (of Pohick)	est. acct.	J	187
George	admr. bond (1836)	Sup. Ct.	111
John	admr. bond	Bond Bk.	123
John	will	M	239
John, Gen'l. (of Clermont)	will	V	295
	inventory	W	66
	sale acct.	W	73, 78
	est. acct.	W	94, 95

Name	Document	Will Book	Page
MASON (continued)			
Mary	will	I	392
Philip	will	D	152
	inventory	D	224
Richard P.	gdn. bond	T	98
Sallie E.	gdn. bond	T	97
Thompson	will	M	130
	inventory	N	387
	est. acct.	N	424
Thompson F.	will	T	1
William	will*		
(of Charles Co.)	inventory*		

MASSERSMITH see MESSERSMITH

MASSEY			
John W.	will	T	225
Lee	will	K	232
Philip	admr. bond	Bond Bk.	172

MASSIE see MASSEY

MASTERSON			
Edward	will	B	69
	inventory	B	76

MATHERS			
Jefferson	will	U	37
	inventory	U	42

MAUZEY			
Ann	gdn. acct.	I	27
	gdn. bond	I	28
Millie	gdn. bond	I	28
	gdn. acct.	I	27
Peter	inventory	H	112, 121
	div. of slaves	H	123
	est. acct.	J	76

Name	Document	Will Book	Page
MAUZEY (continued)			
Priscilla	account	I	27
	inventory	I	511
MAY			
Edward	will (1810 - Alexandria - see FDB L2:228)		
MAYHUE			
Jane	gdn. bond	R	86
MAYSEY			
John	will	B	238
	inventory	B	241
McATEE			
John	will	J	429
	inventory	K	29
	sale acct.	K	30
	est. acct.	K	263
McCARTY			
Daniel	will	F	120
	exor. bond	F	180
	admr. bond	I	33
Dennis	will	A1 pt. 1	13
	admr. bond	A1 pt. 1	14
	inventory	A1 pt. 1	26, 192
	div. of slaves	A1 pt. 1	192
	est. acct.	B	32
Dennis	will	B	152
	acct. vs. George Johnston's est.	B	439
Dennis	gdn. bond	A1 pt. 2	286
Edgar	inventory	N	383
	est. acct.	O	223
John	gdn. bond	I	356

Name	Document	Will Book	Page
McCARTY (continued)			
Mary	will	K	301
	inventory	L	1
Mary Ann	gdn. bond	N	47
Sarah	admr. bond	Sup. Ct.	60
William M.	gdn. bond	J	356
William R.	inventory	N	5
	will	N	149
	bond	N	282
	est. acct.	N	378
	est. acct.	O	220
	est. acct.	P	257
McDANIEL			
John	gdn. bond	S	75
McDONALD			
Alexander	will	F	232
Angus	admr. bond	Bond Bk.	13
Ann	will (1773 - Charles Co., Md.)*		
Henrietta	will (1794)*		
Mary	will	U	242
Robert	will	O	56
	inventory	P	22
	sale acct.	P	25
	est. acct.	P	57
	est. acct.	R	277
	est. acct.	S	302
	div. of slaves	S	348
	est. acct.	T	256
Sarah	will	K	311
Sarah	will	U	240
Valinda	will	K	300
Valinda	will	U	240
McDORMOTT			
Martin	admr. bond	Bond Bk.	166

Name	Document	Will Book	Page
McFARLAND			
Jonathan F.	sale acct.	X	40
	inventory	X	45
	inventory	X	196*
Polly	gdn. bond	F	311
William	admr. bond	Bond Bk.	180
McILHANY			
Mary A.	est. acct.	N	406
McINTEER			
Sarah G.	est. acct.	X	120
William H.	gdn. bond	W	200
McINTOSH			
Catherine	est. acct.	O	50
James	inventory	I	202
John	will	C	55
	inventory	C	57
John	will	L	212
	inventory	O	99
	est. acct.	P	267
McIVER			
Colin	will	E	236b
	inventory	E	273
McKENSIE			
James	inventory	B	296
	admr. bond	Bond Bk.	60
McLAIN			
Samuel	will	F	213
	exor. bond	F	215
	inventory	F	266*
McLEOD			
James	admr. bond	Bond Bk.	86

Name	Document	Will Book	Page
McLURE			
John	admr. bond	Bond Bk.	151
McMAHAN			
Michael	will	E	132
	inventory	E	143
McNALLY			
John	est. acct.	X	48*
MEAD			
Hannah	will	X	369
	inventory	X	399
MEARS			
John	inventory	B	91
	est. acct.	B	193
	admr. bond	Bond Bk.	18
Sinah Ann (nee Allison)	gdn. acct.	V	254
MENDENHALL			
William	will	G	226
	exor. bond	G	227
MESSERSMITH			
Samuel	will	I	274
	inventory	I	314
	debts collected	U	88
	est. acct.	U	212
MIERS			
Jacob	inventory	B	359
	admr. bond	Bond Bk.	65

Name	Document	Will Book	Page

MILLAN

Ann Virginia	gdn. bond	T	65
	gdn. bond	V	1
George	inventory	T	52
	sale acct.	T	58
	list of debts	T	220
	est. acct.	T	252
George W.	gdn. bond	S	539
James	will	T	313
John	will	T	240
	inventory	T	371
	sale acct.	T	373
	est. acct.	V	397
Mary L.	gdn. bond	V	1
Statia (Stacy)	will	T	121
	inventory	T	367
	sale acct.	T	368
	est. acct.	V	396
Thomas	curator's bond	K	228
	will	P	128
	inventory	P	251
	sale acct.	P	252
	est. acct.	Q	223
	est. acct.	R	295
	inventory	T	4
	est. acct.*		
William	will	H	182
	inventory	L	127*
	est. acct.	L	128*
	est. acct.	M	4
William W.	gdn. bond	T	65, 306
	gdn. bond	U	87
	gdn. acct.	U	301*
Willie E.	see WIGGINTON, Willie E.		

Name	Document	Will Book	Page
MILLER			
Mordecai	inventory	Q	335
	will	Sup. Ct.	62
	admr. bond	Sup. Ct.	64
MILLS			
Alexander	will	C	9
	inventory	C	30
	est. acct.	C	189
Daniel	inventory	H	188
Daniel	will	U	380
	inventory	V	216
	sale acct.	V	218
	est. acct.	V	238
	(see also FDB G2:371)		
Edward	gdn. bond	V	72
James	est. acct.	U	411
John	inventory	E	41
	sale acct.	E	50
	list of debts	E	58
John	will	G	384
	inventory	H	26
	sale acct.	J	148
	est. acct.	J	203
Lemuel	inventory	U	444
	sale acct.	U	445
Lemuel	gdn. bond	V	72
Louisa	gdn. bond	U	44
Mahlon	gdn. bond	U	142
Peter	will	O	134*
	inventory	O	395
	inventory	U	121
	sale acct.	U	122
	est. acct.	W	82

Name	Document	Will Book	Page
MILLS (continued)			
Peter	will	X	404
	inventory	Y	28
	inventory	A2	85
	sale acct.	A2	87
	est. acct.	A2	315
Roger	inventory	K	178
	sale acct.	K	317
	widow's dower	K	324
	est. acct.	K	346
Thornton	inventory	U	121
	est. acct.	W	85
Whiting	will	S	266
	inventory	W	315
William	will	P	148
	inventory	R	379
MINOR			
Daniel	inventory	E	197
George	will	I	262
	inventory	I	340
Hugh	gdn. bond	I	267
Jemima	will	I	216
	inventory	I	349
	sale acct.	I	371
	est. acct.	I	419
John	will	B	31
	inventory	B	36
	est. acct.	B	96, 251, 350
	est. acct.	C	89
John	will	D	157
Joseph	est. acct.	V	210
Joseph H.	gdn. bond	K	155
Mary	will (1855 - unprobated)*		
Mildred	est. acct.	Q	334
Nicholas	will	B	362
Thomas Jefferson	gdn. bond	K	147
William	will (1859 - Alexandria)*		

Name	Document	Will Book	Page
MITCHELL			
Benjamin	will	O	51
	inventory	O	148
	sale acct.	R	30
	est. acct.	R	163
	est. acct.	S	153
Elias	admr. bond	A1 pt. 1	98
	inventory	A1 pt. 1	179
Eliza A.	gdn. bond	U	155, 377
	gdn. acct.	V	12
	(in name of Kipps)		
Elizabeth	inventory	R	38
Francis	gdn. acct.	W	329*
Hugh	inventory	S	380
	sale acct.	S	383
	est. acct.	T	355
	est. acct.	U	403
James	gdn. acct.	X	348
Peter	will	X	404
Philo	gdn. acct.	W	332*
William	inventory	P	276
	est. acct.	P	306
	est. acct.	R	167
William H.	gdn. bond	V	391
MIX			
Adeline	gdn. bond	O	102
Emily	gdn. bond	O	102
Lewis	est. acct.	O	382
	est. acct.	P	296
	est. acct.	T	198
Oscar G.	gdn. bond	N	295
	gdn. bond	R	230
	gdn. bond	S	30
	gdn. acct.	S	497
	gdn. acct.	T	195
	gdn. bond	U	75
	gdn. acct.	U	387, 428

Name	Document	Will Book	Page
MOLAN			
Sinah	gdn. bond	F	179
MONEY			
Mary	inventory	R	380
	sale acct.	R	383
Nicholas	will	G	433
	inventory	I	452
	sale acct.	I	454
	est. acct.	I	456
Perry	sale acct.	R	383
MONROE			
Catherine	sale acct.	D	217
George	est. acct.	S	292
	est. acct.	V	197
Jane	will	X	67
John	will	E	105
	est. acct.	E	218
	est. acct.	F	161
	inventory	F	166
Lawrence	will	J	10
	inventory	J	60
Lee H.	inventory	X	318
	sale acct.	X	320
Sarah	will	N	424
	inventory	O	402
	est. acct.	O	413
	est. acct.	P	327
Thomas	inventory	D	132
	est. acct.	D	145
	div. of slaves	D	147
	admr. bond	Bond Bk.	158
MOODY			
Benjamin	will	E	6
	inventory	E	195
	est. acct.	G	243

Name	Document	Will Book	Page
MOODY (continued)			
Samuel	sale acct.	G	192
William	gdn. bond	E	180
MOON(E)			
Mary	gdn. bond	N	148
Patrick	admr. bond	F	218
William	will	I	401
MOORE			
Alfred	gdn. bond	W	210
Annie	gdn. bond	W	210
Arthur	gdn. bond	W	210
Cora	gdn. bond	W	210
Edgar	gdn. bond	W	210
Elizabeth B.	gdn. bond	Q	202
Elizabeth L.	will	W	229
	inventory	W	305
Elmira	gdn. bond	W	210
Florence	gdn. bond	W	210
Francis	will	W	20
	inventory	W	88
Francis	gdn. bond	O	22
Gertrude	gdn. bond	W	210
Henry	will	C	149
	inventory	C	178, 179, 182
Jeremiah	will	K	271
Jeremiah	gdn. bond	O	22
	gdn. bond	W	210
John	will	Q	175
	inventory	Q	236
	sale acct.	Q	359
	est. acct.	R	68, 73, 290
Martha	gdn. bond	O	22
Mary	est. acct.	C	248
	admr. bond	Bond Bk.	132

Name	Document	Will Book	Page
MOORE (continued)			
Nancy P.	will	W	291
	inventory	W	304
Oscar	gdn. bond	W	210
Robert L.	gdn. bond	O	22
Stephen H.	will	K	267
Thomas	gdn. bond	O	22
William	will	C	66
	inventory	C	92
	est. acct.	C	93
	sale acct.	M	252
	est. acct.	M	254
William H.	inventory	W	183
	sale acct.	W	188
	est. acct.	X	123
William S.	est. acct.	U	213, 215
MORGAN			
Enoch	inventory	E	186
Michael	admr. bond	Bond Bk.	26
Mildred	gdn. bond	G	60
MORRIS			
Elizabeth	admr. bond	A1 pt. 2	315
John	will	O	193*
	inventory	O	196, 409
Margaret	will	V	319
MORTON			
Andrew	inventory	D	94
	admr. bond	Bond Bk.	153
Archibald	inventory	I	323
Jane	admr. bond	G	279
	inventory	G	352

Name	Document	Will Book	Page
MOSS			
Ann	will	K	262
Armistead M.	gdn. bond	T	108
	gdn. acct.	U	437
Charles R.	gdn. bond	T	108
	gdn. acct.	U	173
Edgar	gdn. bond	T	109
Emily	gdn. bond	U	84
Evelina Tucker	gdn. bond	R	80
	gdn. acct.	S	306
Gertrude	gdn. bond	R	80
	gdn. acct.	S	306
Horace Holmes	gdn. bond	R	80
	gdn. acct.	S	306
John	will	Sup. Ct.	1
	exor. bond	Sup. Ct.	3
	sale acct.	R	236
	est. acct.	S	146
John T.	gdn. bond	T	110
John William	gdn. bond	R	80
	gdn. acct.	S	306
Juliet	will	T	395
Nancy Boyd	gdn. bond	R	80
Robert	exor. bond	K	52
	will	K	58
	inventory	T	301
Sarah	will	D	67
	est. acct.	D	149
Thomas	will	D	65
	inventory	D	69
	est. acct.	D	150
Thomas	div. of slaves	T	223
	est. acct.	U	233
Virginia	gdn. bond	R	80
	gdn. acct.	S	306

Name	Document	Will Book	Page
MOSS (continued)			
William	inventory	R	353
	sale acct.	S	7
	est. acct.	S	298
MOXLEY			
Daniel	will	B	258
	inventory	B	322
	est. acct.	B	338
James	gdn. bond	A1 pt. 2	394
John	gdn. bond	A1 pt. 2	394
Mary Ann	gdn. bond	A1 pt. 2	394
Richard	inventory	B	188
	est. acct.	B	205, 298
	admr. bond	Bond Bk.	46
Samuel	admr. bond	Bond Bk.	93
Thomas	will	A1 pt. 2	319
	admr. bond	A1 pt. 2	321
	inventory	A1 pt. 2	386
	div. of slaves	A1 pt. 2	463
	sale acct.	A1 pt. 2	527
	est. acct.	A1 pt. 2	527
	est. acct.	B	192
Thomas	will	E	213
	inventory	E	222
Thomas	will	I	36
	sale acct.	O	243
	est. acct.	O	347
William	will	B	1*
	inventory	B	12
MUIR			
George	admr. bond	F	145
	inventory	F	318
James	will	D	196
	inventory	D	345
	sale acct.	D	348

Name	Document	Will Book	Page
MUIR (continued)			
John	will	F	17
	exor. bond	F	18
MUNDAY			
William	inventory	D	256
	will	D	422
	est. acct.	E	66
	admr. bond	Bond Bk.	113
MUNROE see MONROE			
MURPH(E)Y			
Richard	gdn. bond	R	356
Stephen	gdn. bond	R	356
	gdn. bond	T	243
MURRAY			
James	inventory	U	180
Joseph	est. acct.	E	375
Peter	est. acct.	I	7
MUSE			
Priscilla J.	see GANTT, Priscilla J.		
MUSGROVE			
John	will	A1 pt. 1	182
	inventory	A1 pt. 1	202
MYERS			
Jacob	see MIERS, Jacob		
Jane	inventory	I	254
	sale acct.	I	254
NAINBY			
Joseph	admr. bond	F	183
NALLEY			
Elkanah	will	M	183

Name	Document	Will Book	Page
NATION			
William	inventory	B	233
NEALE			
Charles	admr. bond	A1 pt. 1	123
Christopher	inventory	B	243, 375
	est. acct.	B	382, 400
	est. acct.	C	19
	admr. bond	Bond Bk.	43
Christopher	gdn. bond	H	162
Daniel	gdn. acct.	C	13
Hamlet	gdn. bond	I	114
Hamlet	will	J	235
	inventory	J	275
John	admr. bond	Sup. Ct.	9
	inventory	Sup. Ct.	11
Lydia	admr. bond	A1 pt. 1	190
	inventory	A1 pt. 1	199
	est. acct.	A1 pt. 2	517
Presley	will	A1 pt. 2	294
Shapleigh	will	D	36
NELSON			
Sarah	gdn. acct.	A1 pt. 2	518
	gdn. acct.	B	9
	admr. bond	Bond Bk.	47
Thomas	will	Q	108
	inventory	Q	389
	sale acct.	R	39
	est. acct.	R	65
NEWMAN			
Emily A.	gdn. acct.	X	384
Sarah E.	gdn. acct.	X	384
William R.	gdn. acct.	X	384

Name	Document	Will Book	Page
NICHOLAS			
George	will	B	343
	inventory	B	346
	est. acct.	B	362*
NICHOLSON			
Caroline	gdn. bond	J	313
Martha	gdn. bond	J	313
NOLAND			
Charles	est. acct.	L	144*
Christopher	will	I	537
	est. acct.	R	42
Peirce	admr. bond	Bond Bk.	30
NORRIS			
Mariah J.	gdn. bond	K	33
NORTH			
Arelia W.	gdn. bond	L	82
Emily E.	gdn. bond	L	82
George	inventory	K	315
George C.	gdn. bond	L	82
James	inventory	B	389
Jane	admr. bond	Bond Bk.	70
John	inventory	B	132
	est. acct.	B	254
	admr. bond	Bond Bk.	34
Nathaniel G.	gdn. bond	L	82
Thomas J.	gdn. bond	L	82
William D.	gdn. bond	L	82
NORTON			
Richard C.	admr. bond	Sup. Ct.	54
OAKLEY			
Thomas J.	gdn. bond	U	442
	gdn. acct.	V	358

Name	Document	Will Book	Page
OARD			
Thomas	sale acct.	L	78
O'DANIEL			
John	will	G	423
	inventory	H	60
	est. acct.	H	221
	sale acct.	H	223
	est. acct.	J	61
O'DONNELLY			
Patrick	admr. bond	A1 pt. 1	243
O'DRISKEL			
Timothy	inventory	H	241
	sale acct.	I	61
	est. acct.	I	157
OECONOMAS			
Luke	est. acct.	U	402
OFFUTT			
Absolom	will	W	290
	sale acct.	X	21
Alfred D.	gdn. bond	L	94*
	gdn. acct.	N	390
	gdn. acct.	S	45
Hamilton	committee bond	O	60
	sale acct.	O	357
	committee acct.	O	368
	committee bond	S	351
Ozias	inventory	R	20
	sale acct.	R	21
	est. acct.	R	301
Rezin	will	L	55
	inventory	N	15
	est. acct.	O	305

Name	Document	Will Book	Page
OGDON			
Elijah	inventory	M	294
	sale acct.	M	373
	est. acct.	N	234
Matilda	gdn. bond	K	186
Thomas	will	O	165
Thomas	will	T	331
	inventory	T	339
	sale acct.	T	345
	est. acct.	U	409
William	gdn. bond	T	351
O'KEAN			
Henry	will	A1 pt. 1	167
	exor. bond	A1 pt. 1	169
	inventory	A1 pt. 1	180
OLDHAM			
James	inventory	A1 pt. 2	522
OLIVER			
Joseph	sale acct.	H	122
O'MEARA			
Michael	will (Alexandria - see FDB R2:37)		
Thomas Redmond	gdn. bond	Sup. Ct.	35
	gdn. acct.	Sup. Ct.	49, 53, 54, 57, 58
OMOHUNDRA			
Richard	will	A1 pt. 1	129
	exor. bond	A1 pt. 1	131
	inventory	A1 pt. 1	135, 177
O'NEALE			
Charles	inventory	A1 pt. 1	200
	est. acct.	A1 pt. 1	247

Name	Document	Will Book	Page
ORME			
Aaron	inventory	G	61
ORR			
Thomas L.	will	V	228
	sale acct.	X	388
ORTON			
Orrin	will	X	409
OSBORN(E)			
James	will	U	379
	inventory	V	111
	sale acct.	V	114
	est. acct.	V	252
James	gdn. bond	V	148
Richard	will	A1 pt. 2	329
	exor. bond	A1 pt. 2	331
	inventory	A1 pt. 2	448
	sale acct.	A1 pt. 2	454
	est. acct.	A1 pt. 2	476, 516, 531
	est. acct.	B	48, 388, 421
	est. acct.	C	34, 217
Robert	will	A1 pt. 1	33
	exor. bond	A1 pt. 1	34
	inventory	A1 pt. 1	51
	est. acct.	A1 pt. 1	136, 213
OUGHT			
William	admr. bond	Bond Bk.	17
OWENS			
John	inventory	E	218

Name	Document	Will Book	Page
OWSLEY			
Thomas	will	A1 pt. 2	468
	inventory	A1 pt. 2	487, 509
	est. acct.	B	60
PAGE			
Jane Maria	gdn. bond	P	119
William	admr. bond	Bond Bk.	391
	inventory	F	62
PANCOAST			
David	inventory	E	153
PANTON			
John	inventory	K	118
	est. acct.	K	128
	sale acct.	K	134
PARKER			
George	will	Sup. Ct.	61
PARSON(S)			
James	will	E	63
Solomon	vs. Coffer (report)	M	101
	will (1832 - Loudoun Co.)*		
PATTERSON			
Betty	gdn. bond	D	399
Fleming	will	D	82
	inventory	D	139
	sale acct.	E	364
	est. acct.	E	370
John	will	C	35
	inventory	C	80
Susannah	will	G	441
	inventory	H	81
Thomas	exor. bond	F	171
	will	F	172*
	inventory	F	265

Name	Document	Will Book	Page
PATTON			
Robert Jr.	will	O	360
William	admr. bond	Sup. Ct.	125
PAYNE			
Abigail	inventory	N	11
	sale acct.	N	12
	est. acct.	N	13
Asinatte	gdn. bond	R	377
Duvall	gdn. bond	D	427
Elizabeth	gdn. bond	R	377
George	inventory	I	410
	est. acct.	I	475
John	will	J	10
Josias	inventory	D	353
Sanford	will	F	196
	exor. bond	F	198
	inventory	F	305
Sanford	inventory	N	8
	est. acct.	N	9
	sale acct.	N	13
William	will	C	252
	inventory	D	134, 400, 401
	est. acct.	D	136
William	will	D	441
William	will	K	288
	inventory	K	357
	est. acct.	N	172
	inventory	N	365
	sale acct. (see CFF#74ff - Payne vs. Payne - 1836)		
William S.	inventory	W	247
	sale acct.	W	249
	est. acct.	W	275

PEABODY see PEEBODY

Name	Document	Will Book	Page
PEACOCK			
Hezekiah	inventory	X	322
	sale acct.	X	325
PEAKE			
Humphrey	will	E	91
Mary	inventory	J	44
	sale acct.	J	48
	est. acct.	J	49
William	will	B	247
	inventory	B	260
William Jr.	will	B	105
	inventory	B	123
William	will	G	10
	exor. bond	G	12
	inventory	G	73
PEARSON			
Mary Jane (nee Follin)	gdn. acct.	U	432
Robert F.	inventory	V	363
	sale acct.	W	195
Samuel	inventory	B	30
	est. acct.	B	50
	admr. bond	Bond Bk.	2, 8
Simon, Capt.	will (1731 - Stafford Co.)		
	est. acct.	A1 pt. 1	149, 201, 252
	est. acct.	A1 pt. 2	361, 495, 530
Simon	gdn. bond	A1 pt. 1	144
Simon	will	G	356
Thomas	will	A1 pt. 1	65
	exor. bond	A1 pt. 1	65
	inventory	A1 pt. 1	71
	est. acct.	A1 pt. 1	101
William M.	est. acct.	W	14

Name	Document	Will Book	Page
PEEBODY			
John	will	E	32
	inventory	E	38
	est. acct.	E	99
PETER			
Martha	gdn. acct.	I	283
	gdn. acct.	K	121
Martha	see also CUSTIS, Martha (Patsy)		
Thomas	gdn. acct.	I	283
PETTITT			
John	inventory	D	15, 200
	est. acct.	D	201
	admr. bond	Bond Bk.	134
PEYRONIE			
William	inventory	B	95
	est. acct.	B	104
	admr. bond	Bond Bk.	24
PEYTON			
Valentine	will	G	182
	exor. bond	G	183
	inventory	J	430
	est. acct.	J	433
PHILLIPS			
John	will	B	94
John	will	G	357
	sale acct.	G	411
	inventory	G	418
	est. acct.	H	86
PIMMITT			
Edward	will	A1 pt. 2	468
	inventory	A1 pt. 2	479

Name	Document	Will Book	Page
PIMMITT (continued)			
George	will	A1 pt. 1	46
	exor. bond	A1 pt. 1	48
	inventory	A1 pt. 1	54
Moses	will	A1 pt. 2	338
	exor. bond	A1 pt. 2	339
Sarah	will	A1 pt. 1	262
	exor. bond	A1 pt. 1	263
	inventory	A1 pt. 2	283
PINKSTONE			
Greenberry	inventory	C	129
	admr. bond	Bond Bk.	109
PIPER			
David	inventory	B	414
	admr. bond	Bond Bk.	73
Harry	will	D	162
Henry	will	K	35
POOLE			
Edward	est. acct.	R	159
	inventory	S	71
	est. acct.	S	181
PORTER			
Sinah B.	will (1853 - Alexandria Co.)*		
POTTER			
James	inventory	X	82
	sale acct.	X	142
	est. acct.	X	422
Joseph	will	I	231
POULTNEY			
Richard	admr. bond	A1 pt. 1	205
	inventory	A1 pt. 1	247

Name	Document	Will Book	Page
POWELL			
Beverly	gdn. bond	O	55
	will	U	350
	sale acct.	V	109
	est. acct.	V	109
Bushrod	gdn. bond	O	81
	will	T	115
	inventory	T	179
Cuthbert	will	W	278
Edmund	gdn. bond	O	70
Jane Eliza	gdn. acct.	S	318
John	will	N	182
	sale acct.	N	381
	inventory	O	90
	curator's bond	S	74
Joseph	will	I	217
	inventory	I	257
	est. acct.	J	428
Joseph	will	K	374
	inventory	K	412
	inventory	O	86
	sale acct.	O	374
	est. acct.	O	423
	inventory	P	177
	est. acct.	P	328
	est. acct.	Q	121
	est. acct.	S	283
Joseph	gdn. acct.	S	318
Lucinda	gdn. bond	O	80
	gdn. acct.	S	318
Micajah	admr. bond	Bond Bk.	75
Susannah	inventory	O	88
	sale acct.	O	373
	est. acct.	P	68
	est. acct.	Q	117

Name	Document	Will Book	Page
POWELL (continued)			
William Sr.	will	I	144
	inventory	I	220
	sale acct.	I	224
	est. acct.	M	220
POWER			
James	will	A1 pt. 1	127
PRATT			
Shubael	will	E	113
	inventory	E	139
PRESCOTT			
John	inventory	C	245
	admr. bond	Bond Bk.	131
PRESGRAVE			
Jeremiah	inventory	A1 pt. 2	525
	sale acct.	A1 pt. 2	526
	est. acct.	A1 pt. 2	526
PRESTON			
Robert	will	B	175
PRICE			
David	admr. bond	Bond Bk.	62
David	will	E	62
	inventory	E	79
John	will	E	127
PRITCHART			
Lewis	inventory	I	226
Lewis	gdn. bond	Q	31
	gdn. acct.	R	87
Mary	gdn. bond	Q	30
	gdn. acct.	R	85

Name	Document	Will Book	Page
PRITCHART (continued)			
Sarah	inventory	N	60
	sale acct.	N	229
Travis	inventory	N	372
	sale acct.	O	112
	est. acct.	Q	39
PROUT			
Henry G.	gdn. bond	V	125
Mary B.	gdn. bond	V	125
William	admr. bond	Sup. Ct.	133
	inventory	V	134
	sale acct.	V	136
PURLEY			
Ann	trustee acct.	T	18
PYLE			
David	will	E	298
	exor. bond	E	299
	inventory	E	346
QUAIGLEY see QUIGLEY			
QUIGLEY			
Anastasia	will	U	433
RAINES			
John	will	B	84
	inventory	B	90
RAMEY			
Benjamin	est. acct.	A1 pt. 2	520
RAMSAY			
Amelia	gdn. bond	E	103, 128
	admr. bond	F	89

Name	Document	Will Book	Page

RAMSEY (continued)
Ann	inventory	E	112
Anthony	inventory	B	42
	admr. bond	Bond Bk.	6
		Bond Bk.	127
John	inventory	E	24
John	will	M	273
William	will	E	69
	inventory	E	107

RANES see RAINES

RATCLIFFE
Ann Maria	gdn. bond	O	274
Barbara	will	G	220
	exor. bond	G	221
Charles	will	Sup. Ct.	104
	admr. bond	Sup. Ct.	105
Charlotte F.	gdn. bond	P	1, 168
	gdn. acct.	P	269
	(in name of Helm)		
John	admr. bond	G	305
John	est. acct.	M	420
	inventory	N	64
	sale acct.	N	67
Marion B.	gdn. bond	S	540
Richard	will	O	57*
	inventory	P	395
	sale acct.	P	398
	est. acct.	R	11, 14
Sarah	gdn. bond	F	290
	(see also FDB R1:93)		

READ see REID

REAGAN
Michael	will	C	187
	inventory	C	213
	will	E	10

Name	Document	Will Book	Page
REAGAN (continued)			
Peter	admr. bond	Bond Bk.	21
William	inventory	B	49
	est. acct.	B	80
	admr. bond	Bond Bk.	14
REARDON			
John	gdn. bond	E	273
John	inventory	D	86
	est. acct.	F	169
	admr. bond	Bond Bk.	165
John B.	will	W	292
Yelverton	will	Sup. Ct.	22*
	exor. bond	Sup. Ct.	23
REDMON			
Thomas	will (1801 - Alexandria - see FDB E2:213)		
REED see REID			
REGAN see REAGAN			
REID			
Ann	will	T	94
	div. of slaves	T	131
	est. acct.	U	62
Ann E.	gdn. bond	62	390
Catherine	gdn. bond	I	310
Catherine T.	gdn. bond	T	7
Charles J.	gdn. acct.	X	57*
Eliza	trustee acct.	U	104
Hugh	admr. bond	Bond Bk.	177
James	will	Q	51
James L.	gdn. acct.	X	57*
Jane	inventory	I	376
Jesse	gdn. bond	I	310

Name	Document	Will Book	Page
REID (continued)			
John	inventory	S	270
	est. acct.	T	49
John N.	gdn. bond	P	125
	inventory	W	344*
	sale acct.	W	345*
	est. acct.	X	197*
Joseph	will	A1 pt. 2	325
	exor. bond	A1 pt. 2	326
	inventory	A1 pt. 2	364, 466
	est. acct.	B	124
Lucretia M.	gdn. bond	T	7
Martha H.	gdn. bond	V	390
Mary	gdn. bond	T	7
Patrick J.	will	W	202
	inventory	X	177
	sale acct.	X	179
Robert S.	will	U	33
	inventory	U	40
	sale acct.	U	41
	est. acct.	V	354
Sarah Ellen	gdn. bond	V	390
Thomas	will	F	316
	admr. bond	F	344
	inventory	G	25
	sale acct.	G	27
	div. of slaves	G	232
	est. acct.	G	351
Thomas	gdn. bond	G	292
William	gdn. bond	G	292
REMINGTON			
Absolom	inventory	W	127
	est. acct.	W	146
Ann M.	gdn. bond	W	155
Charles G.	gdn. bond	W	155
Richard H.	gdn. bond	W	155

Name	Document	Will Book	Page
REMINGTON (continued)			
Susan R.	gdn. bond	W	155
Virginia C.	gdn. bond	W	155
William F.	gdn. bond	W	155
REMNANT			
John	will	E	198
RICHARDS			
Ann	gdn. bond	I	179
Barton	gdn. bond	I	179
Benjamin	admr. bond	A1 pt. 1	197
	inventory	A1 pt. 1	209
	est. acct.	A1 pt. 1	209
George	admr. bond	E	323
James	will	K	313
	inventory	K	404
James	est. acct.	L	328
	est. acct.	N	340
	est. acct.	S	347
John, Dr.	will (1843 - Alexandria)*		
William	inventory	I	497
	inventory	J	7
	sale acct.	J	9
William	will	K	69
	inventory	K	206
	est. acct.	L	141*
RICHARDSON			
John	will	A1 pt. 1	131
	exor. bond	A1 pt. 1	132
	inventory	A1 pt. 1	155
RICHSTER			
John	will	K	95

Name	Document	Will Book	Page
RICKETTS			
David	inventory	Q	417
	est. acct.	R	126
RICKSEY			
William	will	A1 pt. 2	507
RIDDELL			
Andrew	admr. bond	Bond Bk.	67
RIDDLE			
Robert	will	M	232
	est. acct.	O	372
RIGDON			
Edward	will	C	136*
	inventory	C	139
	est. acct.	D	271
RIGG			
John	will	V	305
	inventory	V	377
	sale acct.	V	380
	est. acct.	W	137
Sarah	will	O	411
	sale acct.	P	33
	inventory	P	37
	est. acct.	P	412
	est. acct.	Q	41

RIXEY see RICKSEY

ROACH			
George	inventory	N	371

Name	Document	Will Book	Page
ROBERDEAU			
James M.	will	Q	245
	inventory	Q	375
	sale acct.	Q	378
	est. acct.	R	287
Jane E.	gdn. bond	Q	276
	gdn. acct.	U	79
ROBERT			
Samuel	admr. bond	G	184
ROBERTS			
John	will	A1 pt. 2	313
	exor. bond	A1 pt. 2	315
	inventory	A1 pt. 2	433
ROBERTSON			
George	will	D	295
	inventory	D	361
	sale acct.	D	363
	est. acct.	E	25, 169, 253, 403
	est. acct.	F	327
	est. acct.	G	50
James	will	C	47
	accounts (1731 - 1745)*		
James	gdn. bond	E	359
John	admr. bond	F	141
Joseph	will	E	137
	inventory	E	165
Thomas	admr. bond	A1 pt. 1	118
	inventory	B	18, 19
	est. acct.	B	20
William	gdn. bond	G	179
William	will	K	405
	inventory	L	102*

Name	Document	Will Book	Page

RODGERS see ROGERS

ROGERS

Arthur L.	gdn. bond	V	331
Hugh H.	gdn. bond	V	331
John D.	gdn. bond	V	331
Laura F.	gdn. bond	V	331
Lucy D.	gdn. bond	V	331
Richard	admr. bond	A1 pt. 1	9
	inventory	A1 pt. 1	11
	est. acct.	A1 pt. 1	24
Robert	will	S	456
	sale acct.	T	192
	est. acct.	T	193
William	admr. bond	F	216
	inventory	F	286
William	will	K	184
	inventory	K	345
	est. acct.	L	143*

ROLLINGS

Elizabeth	inventory	B	160
John	inventory	E	104

ROSE

Alexander M.	gdn. bond	S	265
Ann Washington	renounces provisions of		
	husband's will	J	337
Augustin	gdn. bond	S	265
Catherine	will	J	120
	inventory	J	305
Henry	will	I	262
	inventory	J	308
John	admr. bond	A1 pt. 1	103
John	inventory	J	297
Susan A.	gdn. bond	S	265
William	gdn. bond	S	265

Name	Document	Will Book	Page
ROUZEE			
Julia Ann	will	V	323
ROWLES			
Joseph E.	inventory	K	3
	admr. bond	N	291
Julia Ann	gdn. bond	K	25, 297
	gdn. acct.	L	108*
	gdn. acct.	N	344
ROWSE			
Thomas	will	M	64
RUMNEY			
William	will	D	424
RUSSELL			
Charles	inventory	I	507
RYAN			
James	inventory	R	217
	sale acct.	R	218
	est. acct.	R	325
William P.	inventory	W	22
	sale acct.	W	26
	est. acct.	W	233
	est. acct.	X	64*
ST. CLAIR			
Henry Clay	gdn. bond	T	232
	gdn. acct.	X	230
Julia Ann E.	gdn. bond	T	232
	gdn. acct.	X	226
Margaret	will (1764 - Loudoun Co. WB A:115)		
Robert W.	gdn. bond	T	232
	gdn. bond	U	320
	gdn. acct.	W	147
	gdn. acct.	X	222

Name	Document	Will Book	Page

ST. CLAIR see also SINCLAIR

SALKELD

Henry	inventory	B	93
	est. acct.	B	167, 376
	admr. bond	Bond Bk.	25

SANDERS see SAUNDERS

SANDFORD see SANFORD

SANFORD

Edward	will	K	214
	inventory	K	217
	inventory	L	172*
Joseph	inventory	S	53
	sale acct.	S	54
	est. acct.	S	179
Margaret	will	L	187
Richard	will	G	440
Robert	will	C	70
	inventory	C	71

SANGSTER

Alexander	gdn. bond	G	320
	gdn. bond	I	181
George	gdn. bond	G	319
James	sale acct.	T	343
	est. acct.	U	51
Mary	gdn. bond	G	320
Robert	gdn. bond	G	219
Thomas	gdn. bond	G	219
Thomas	admr. bond	G	217
	inventory	G	338
	sale acct.	G	340
	est. acct.	J	198

Name	Document	Will Book	Page
SAUNDERS			
Adeline	gdn. bond	S	105
	gdn. acct.	X	284
Ann	gdn. bond	N	48
Daniel	will	T	228
	inventory	U	141
Elizabeth	inventory	R	343
	sale acct.	R	346
	admr. acct.*		
John	inventory	N	87
	sale acct.	N	91
Joseph	will	F	251
(of Philadelphia)			
Mary Catharine	gdn. bond	S	105
	gdn. acct.	X	284
William G.	gdn. bond	Sup. Ct.	110
SAVEN			
Nicholas	admr. bond	Bond Bk.	16
SAWKINS			
James	inventory	J	145
SCANLIN			
Thomas	inventory	A1 pt. 1	207
	est. acct.	A1 pt. 1	236
SCISSON			
John B.	gdn. bond	P	425
SCOTT			
Alexander	gdn. bond	E	121
James	admr. bond	G	9
James H.	inventory	X	311
	sale acct.	X	313
John M.	gdn. bond	Sup. Ct.	126
Mary	gdn. bond	Q	49
	gdn. bond	R	184

Name	Document	Will Book	Page
SCOTT (continued)			
Richard Marshall	gdn. bond	R	184
	gdn. bond	Sup. Ct.	137
Richard Marshall	admr. bond	Sup. Ct.	72
	will	Sup. Ct.	79
	exor. bond	Sup. Ct.	127
	admr. bond	Sup. Ct.	131
Ruth (nee Fish)	inventory	W	313
	sale acct.	W	316
	curator's acct.	X	373
	admr. bond	Sup. Ct.	157
Sabret	will	O	77
	inventory	P	139
	est. acct.	Q	207
Thomas	inventory	C	62
	admr. bond	Bond Bk.	97
William	will	E	232*
	inventory	F	25
William B.	gdn. bond	I	457
SCRIVENER			
Nancy	gdn. bond	E	243
SEARS			
William	will	I	436
William B.	will	L	197
SEBASTIAN			
Benjamin	will	C	95
	inventory	C	130, 190
Benjamin, Rev.	will* (1834 - Breckinridge Co., Ky.)		
Elizabeth	will	C	216
Nancy	will	N	134
Narcissa	gdn. bond	L	78
	gdn. acct.	M	248
	gdn. acct.	Q	33, 38
Priscilla	admr. bond	Bond Bk.	114
	est. acct.	T	217

Name	Document	Will Book	Page
SELECTMAN			
George	inventory	T	13
	sale acct.	T	15
SELEVEN			
John	will	B	39
SEWALL see SEWELL			
SEWELL			
Amanda	gdn. bond	R	378
Franklin L.	gdn. bond	S	388
	gdn. acct.	T	182
	gdn. acct.	U	10
	gdn. acct.	V	333
John F.	gdn. bond	S	352
	gdn. acct.	S	410
	gdn. acct.	T	248
	gdn. bond	U	89
	gdn. acct.	U	57, 158, 429
Joseph	will	R	373
	inventory	R	393
	sale acct.	R	397
	est. acct.	S	402, 510
	est. acct.	T	246
	est. acct.	U	54, 106
Joseph W.	gdn. bond	R	377
William	inventory	C	111
	admr. bond	Bond Bk.	105
SHAW			
Jane	will	C	41
John	inventory	D	337
Thomas	will	D	38
	inventory	D	75
	est. acct.	D	197

Name	Document	Will Book	Page
SHAW (continued)			
William	will	C	223
	inventory	D	11, 339
	sale acct.	D	12, 342
SHEARMAN			
John B.	admr. bond	Sup. Ct.	162
SHEARMAN see also SHERMAN			
SHEEHY			
James	will	L	221
SHELLY			
John	will	K	262
	est. acct.	S	107
SHEPPARD			
Charlotte	committee bond	K	289
	committee acct.	N	352
Eliza	gdn. bond	L	48
	will	W	119
	est. acct.	W	327*
Israel J.	gdn. bond	L	48
John	admr. bond	I	13
	inventory	I	55
	est. acct.	L	100
Sarah Ann	gdn. bond	L	48
	sale acct.	R	349
	inventory	R	360
William	inventory	L	40
	sale acct.	L	44
	est. acct.	L	101*
William	gdn. bond	L	48
SHERIDAN			
John	will	C	29
	inventory	C	40

Name	Document	Will Book	Page
SHERIFF			
Thomas	will	X	72
	inventory	X	77
SHERMAN			
Peter	inventory	O	115
	sale acct.	O	118
	est. acct.	O	319
	est. acct.	Q	116
SHERMAN see also SHEARMAN			
SHINN			
Adam	admr. bond	G	133
SHORES			
Richard	will	A1 pt. 2	458
	inventory	A1 pt. 2	510
	est. acct.	A1 pt. 2	512
	est. acct.	B	215
SHORTRIDGE			
William	inventory	D	360
SHREVE			
Daniel	exor. bond	A1 pt. 2	345, 388
	will	A1 pt. 2	403
	inventory	A1 pt. 2	410
	est. acct.	A1 pt. 2	516
William	admr. bond	A1 pt. 2	398
	inventory	A1 pt. 2	409
	sale acct.	A 1 pt. 2	513
	est. acct.	A1 pt. 2	514
SIBLEY			
John	will	A1 pt. 2	382
	exor. bond	A1 pt. 2	392
	inventory	A1 pt. 2	437
	est. acct.	B	56, 57

Name	Document	Will Book	Page
SIMMONS			
Elizabeth	inventory	K	51
	est. acct.	L	99*
James	admr. bond	A1 pt. 2	311
Thomas	will	A1 pt. 1	90
	exor. bond	A1 pt. 1	90
	inventory	A1 pt. 1	93
SIM(M)S			
Behethlem	gdn. bond	R	369
Humphrey	will	P	346
Mary Ann	gdn. bond	R	369
Mary Jane	gdn. bond	R	369
Nancy	gdn. bond	R	369
	gdn. bond	U	325
SIMONS			
Ann	will	C	23
SIMPSON			
Alexander E.	gdn. bond	U	38
Ann	committee bond	M	75
	inventory	N	313
	committee acct.	N	315
	est. acct.	O	235, 353
	committee acct.	O	345
	est. acct.	P	231
Catherine	will	N	194
	est. acct.	O	205
Catherine W.	gdn. bond	L	381
	gdn. bond	M	129, 275
Edward F.	gdn. bond	L	381
Frances	gdn. bond	U	38
French	admr. bond	G	115
George	will	D	292
	inventory	E	123

Name	Document	Will Book	Page
SIMPSON (continued)			
George	inventory	K	11
	est. acct.	M	52
	inventory	M	56
	inventory	O	106
	sale acct.	O	108
	est. acct.	O	239, 391
	est. acct.	P	941, 207
George B.	inventory	U	131
	sale acct.	U	133
Gilbert	will	C	188
Gilbert	will	I	260
Gilbert	will	J	218
James	will	I	420
	inventory	J	2
	est. acct.	K	171
	inventory	N	246
	sale acct.	N	250
James	inventory of slaves	W	227
James	gdn. bond	L	381
	gdn. bond	O	61
Jane	est. acct.	N	311
	est. acct.	P	42
Jane	gdn. acct.	U	414
Jane Elizabeth	gdn. bond	O	147
John	gdn. bond	D	335
	gdn. bond	G	189
John	will	J	150
John	will	N	277
	sale acct.	O	103
	est. acct.	O	205
Joseph	gdn. bond	O	61
Joseph	will	G	230
	exor. bond	G	239
	inventory	H	92
	inventory	N	35
	sale acct.	N	73

Name	Document	Will Book	Page
SIMPSON (continued)			
Joseph (cont'd)	est. acct.	N	346
	est. acct.	P	62
Josias	will	T	178
	inventory	T	390
Judith	gdn. bond	L	381
Matilda C.	gdn. bond	U	38
Moses	admr. bond	Bond Bk.	170
	inventory	D	208
	div. of slaves	D	222
Moses	will	E	184
	inventory	F	206
	est. acct.	F	210
	est. acct.	G	334
	est. acct.	H	233
	est. acct.	M	65
	sale acct.	M	222
Moses	inventory	S	354
	sale acct.	S	372
	est. acct.	T	153
Nancy	gdn. bond	P	240
Nancy A.	will	W	129
	inventory	W	224
	sale acct.	W	225
	committee acct.	X	277
	est. acct.	X	277
	est. acct. (1860)*		
Richard	will	B	347
	inventory	B	351
	est. acct.	C	33
Richard	inventory	M	102
	sale acct.	M	112
	est. acct.	O	226, 313
	est. acct.	P	88, 236
	est. acct.	U	156
Robert W.	gdn. bond	W	223

Name	Document	Will Book	Page
SIMPSON (continued)			
Sarah	will	B	418
	inventory	B	434
Sibyl	admr. bond	F	155
	inventory	F	184
Silas	will	P	118
Spencer	est. acct.	J	328
Susannah	gdn. bond	N	29
Susannah	inventory	M	56
Thomas	will	M	229
Thomas	will (1734 - Pr. Wm. Co. WB C:16)*		
(of Pr. Wm. Co.)	admr. bond*		
	inventory*		
Thompson	est. acct.	U	66
William	inventory	H	144
	sale acct.	H	145
	est. acct.	H	147
	admr. bond	H	197
William	inventory	M	342
	sale acct.	M	349
	admr. bond	N	133
	est. acct.	N	150
	est. acct.	P	42
SINCLAIR			
Amos	will	A1 pt. 1	76
	admr. bond	A1 pt. 1	77
	inventory	A1 pt. 1	86
Elizabeth	gdn. bond	S	76
Jane	gdn. bond	S	76
Jane	will	R	322
John	gdn. bond	S	73
Lemuel G.	will	S	93
	inventory	S	218
Thomas	will	L	209
	inventory	L	368
Thomas	gdn. bond	S	76

Name	Document	Will Book	Page
SINCLAIR (continued)			
Thomas B.	inventory	S	26
	sale acct.	S	31
	est. acct.	S	294, 442
William	gdn. bond	S	73
Zippora	will	S	75
	inventory	S	83
	sale acct.	S	86
	est. acct.	S	441

SINCLAIR see also ST.CLAIR

SINKLER see ST.CLAIR, SINCLAIR

SISSON see SCISSON

SKIDMORE			
John	will	V	71
SKINNER			
Elizabeth	gdn. bond	L	196
Samuel	gdn. bond	L	196
William	will	U	45
	inventory	U	82
	sale acct.	U	83
SLAUGHTER			
Ann	will	G	412
	inventory	G	443
SLY			
Richard	admr. bond	A1 pt. 1	113
	inventory	A1 pt. 1	125
SMITH			
Ann Elizabeth	gdn. bond	Sup. Ct.	134

Name	Document	Will Book	Page
SMITH (continued)			
Augustine J.	inventory	Q	11
	sale acct.	Q	160
	est. acct.	Q	252
Charles	inventory	P	347
	debts	P	360
	will	P	410
	sale acct.	P	416
	div. of slaves	Q	240
	est. acct.	Q	249
Charles B.	gdn. bond	T	338
Eliza	inventory	U	92
	sale acct.	U	95
	est. acct.	X	435
	est. acct. (see CFF#30v - Fairfax) vs. Smith - 1843)		
George	est. acct.	P	361
Gustin	gdn. bond	T	338
Gustin B.	curator's bond	K	230
	inventory	Q	297
Jacob	admr. bond	A1 pt. 2	396
	will	A1 pt. 2	404
	inventory	A1 pt. 2	411
	est. acct.	B	40
	inventory	B	54
James	will	A1 pt. 2	480
	inventory	A1 pt. 2	519
James	inventory	I	450
	est. acct.	L	118*
James L.	est. acct.	P	361
Jane	gdn. bond	P	420
Jane	will	U	170
Joseph	will	N	212
Keron H.	est. acct.	P	361
Lane	gdn. bond	J	73
Margaret	will	C	244
	est. acct.	D	44

Name	Document	Will Book	Page
SMITH (continued)			
Mary Ann	inventory	Q	298
	sale acct.	Q	300
	est. acct.	R	284
	est. acct.	S	201
Mary Virginia	gdn. bond	Sup. Ct.	134
Nathaniel	ordinary bond	A1 pt. 2	298
Robert J. T.	gdn. bond	P	423
Sabina	inventory	T	56
	sale acct.	T	69
	est. acct.	V	393
Sallie Ann	will	V	3
	inventory	V	361
	sale acct.	V	393
Samuel	will	H	25
Samuel	will	T	10
	exor. bond	T	12
	inventory	T	50
	inventory	U	90
	sale acct.	U	93
	est. acct. (see CFF#30v - Fairfax vs. Smith - 1843)		
Susannah	will	S	92
Temple	will	P	272
Temple	gdn. bond.	R	332
	will	W	80
	inventory	W	162
	sale acct.	W	165
	est. acct.	X	361
Thomas	will	B	374
	inventory	B	379, 381
William	gdn. bond	T	338
William	will	A1 pt. 2	478
	inventory	A1 pt. 2	491
	inventory	B	145
	admr. bond	Bond Bk.	42

Name	Document	Will Book	Page
SMITH (continued)			
William	inventory	E	155
	will	E	234
	est. acct.	E	319, 320
William	will (Loudoun Co. - see FDB R2:346)		
William F.	gdn. bond	P	423
SOMERS see **SUMMERS**			
SONGSTER see **SANGSTER**			
SPARKS			
Jeremiah	admr. bond	A1 pt. 2	389
SPEAKE			
Lucretia	will	L	95*
SPENCE			
Henry	inventory	V	226
John	inventory	B	225
	est. acct.	B	407
	admr. bond	Bond Bk.	54
Maria	gdn. bond	V	66
SPINDLE			
James Madison	gdn. bond	O	365
William Edward	gdn. bond	O	366
SPINKS			
Enoch	gdn. acct.	E	68
John	will	D	99
	inventory	D	105
SPURLING			
Jeremiah	est. acct.	L	149*
John	inventory	J	79
	est. acct.	J	138

Name	Document	Will Book	Page
STAFFORD			
William	admr. bond	A1 pt. 2	421
	inventory	A1 pt. 2	463
	sale acct.	A1 pt. 2	479
STANHOPE			
Ann	will	S	106
	div. of slaves	T	239
	admr. acct.	T	262
Eliza J.	gdn. bond	R	371
Frances L.	gdn. bond	T	106, 389
	gdn. acct.	U	16
	gdn. bond	U	45
	gdn. acct.	W	355*
John	inventory	R	246
John W.	gdn. bond	T	106, 389
	gdn. acct.	U	16
	gdn. bond	U	45
	gdn. acct.	W	355*
Lewis G.	gdn. bond	S	217
	gdn. acct.	T	244
Lewis R.	admr. acct.*		
Margaret A.	gdn. bond	T	106, 389
	gdn. acct.	U	16
	gdn. bond	U	45
	gdn. acct.	W	352*
William	gdn. bond	I	40
William	admr. bond	I	53
	inventory	I	100
William H.	will	S	105
	inventory	S	483
STEEL			
John	admr. bond	Bond Bk.	117
Mary	will	V	222

STEUART see STEWART, STUART

Name	Document	Will Book	Page
STEWART			
Andrew	will	D	47
Benjamin	admr. bond	F	224
Branham Augusta	gdn. bond	V	149, 332
	gdn. acct.	W	13, 241, 362*
	gdn. bond	W	178
	gdn. acct.	X	437
Caroline E.	gdn. bond	V	149, 332
	gdn. acct.	W	13, 241, 362*
	gdn. bond	W	178
	gdn. acct.	X	437
Frances Ann	gdn. bond	V	149, 332
	gdn. acct.	W	13, 241, 362*
	gdn. bond	W	178
	gdn. acct.	X	437
James	will	D	235
	inventory	D	428
John	inventory	I	97
John B.	inventory	V	35
	sale acct.	V	41
	est. acct.	V	235

STEWART see also **STUART**

Name	Document	Will Book	Page
STONE			
Caleb Sr.	inventory	N	183
	sale acct.	N	188
	est. acct.	O	249
	est. acct.	P	64
Caleb F.	inventory	W	131
	sale acct.	W	133
	est. acct.	W	340*
Charles S.	gdn. bond	W	180
Daniel	will	K	199

Name	Document	Will Book	Page
STONE (continued)			
Eli	will	F	54
	exor. bond	F	56
	inventory	F	153
	est. acct.	F	294
Jane	will	S	537
	inventory	T	83
	sale acct.	T	85
	est. acct.	T	364
John	inventory	D	214
	admr. bond	Bond Bk.	149
Levi	will	N	283
	inventory	R	95
	sale acct.	R	97, 168
Olivia	will	N	269
Samuel	will	E	77
Samuel	will	I	154
STORTS			
Henry	inventory	J	176
STRICTLAND			
William	admr. bond	Bond Bk.	173
STUART			
Charles Calvert	admr. bond	Sup. Ct.	140
	inventory	Sup. Ct.	143
	sale acct.	Sup. Ct.	147
David, Dr.	will	K	238
	inventory	K	244
	est. acct.	Q	214
William Sholto	will	M	386
	est. acct.	R	304

STUART see also STEWART

Name	Document	Will Book	Page
STUBBLEFIELD			
Thomas	inventory	E	69
	est. acct.	E	172
STUCKBERRY			
Robert	admr. bond	A1 pt. 2	416
	inventory	A1 pt. 2	475
STURMAN			
William	admr. bond	A1 pt. 1	181
	inventory	A1 pt. 1	188
SUDDATH			
Benjamin	will	F	156
	exor. bond	F	158
	inventory	G	28
Cassandra	will	V	65
James G.	inventory	P	341
	sale acct.	P	343
	est. acct.	Q	231
	est. acct.	V	350
Lewis	inventory	T	231
	sale acct.	T	232
	will	U	111
SULLIVAN			
Daniel	admr. bond	G	265
	sale acct.	G	348
Mary T.	inventory	P	241
	sale acct.	R	37
	est. acct.	R	165
SUMMERS			
Ann	gdn. bond	I	406
Elizabeth	will	N	34
	inventory	O	10
	est. acct.	O	17
	sale acct.	O	31
	est. acct.	R	263

Name	Document	Will Book	Page
SUMMERS (continued)			
Francis	will	H	171
Francis	gdn. bond	I	407
George, Col.	admr. bond	I	64
	inventory	I	366
	sale acct.	J	64*
	est. acct.	J	64*
George	inventory	T	234
	sale acct.	T	236
Jane	will	K	254
John	will	E	238
	inventory	E	342
	est. acct.	G	362
John	will	M	298
	inventory	M	326
	inventory	O	11
	est. acct.	O	16, 733
	sale acct.	O	26
	est. acct.	p	4
	est. acct.	Q	60
	est. acct.	R	27, 263, 307
	est. acct.	S	342
	est. acct.	T	26
Mary	will	J	219
	inventory	J	395
	sale acct.	K	190
	est. acct.	K	197
Simon	will	N	82
William	will	H	31
	inventory	H	149
	est. acct.	J	179
William	will (1797 - Alexandria)*		
William Thomas	gdn. bond	Sup. Ct.	102
SUTHERLAND			
Mary	inventory	T	393
	sale acct.	U	32

Name	Document	Will Book	Page
SUTTLE			
Baily	inventory	H	139
SUTTON			
Alfred	sale acct.	V	126
	inventory	V	133
	est. acct.	V	278
SWARTWOUT			
William	inventory	T	380
	sale acct.	T	384
	est. acct.	U	162
SWEENEY			
George W.	gdn. bond	R	133
	gdn. acct.	X	62*
Sarah E.	gdn. acct.	X	62*
SWINK			
Frances Ann	gdn. bond	U	46*
George	est. acct.	U	163
George W.	gdn. bond	W	154
John	will	O	400
	est. acct.	S	286, 287
	inventory	T	102
John William	gdn. bond	U	46*
Joseph S.	gdn. bond	P	82
	inventory	T	291
	sale acct.	T	293
Josephine	gdn. bond	U	46*
Mary	inventory	O	325
Mary Jane	gdn. bond	P	41
Salome	will	R	375
	inventory	S	244
	est. acct.	U	64
Sarah Ann	est. acct.	W	273, 363*
William	will	M	335
	inventory	O	326

Name	Document	Will Book	Page
SYDNOR			
Ellen	will	J	103
TALBERT see TALBOTT			
TALBOTT			
Benjamin	inventory	I	439
	est. acct.	J	33
	est. acct.	L	413
Benjamin (son of Polly)	gdn. bond	K	423
Daniel	inventory	D	119
	est. acct.	D	128
	admr. bond	Bond Bk.	160
Martha	gdn. bond	K	420
Mary	inventory	L	407
	sale acct.	L	411
	est. acct.	L	414
Mary Magdalene	will	F	22
	exor. bond	F	38
	inventory	F	83
	est. acct.	F	86
Ozborn	inventory	E	268
	est. acct.	G	357
Samuel	inventory	D	109
	sale acct.	D	113
	est. acct.	D	115
	widow's dower allotted	D	116
	admr. bond	Bond Bk.	163
Sarah	gdn. bond	K	420
Thomas	exor. bond	Sup. Ct.	136
	will	Sup. Ct.	139
William R.	gdn. bond	W	156
William Smith	will	L	109*

TANKERVILLE, Earl of see BENNETT, Charles

Name	Document	Will Book	Page
TAREN			
Robert	admr. bond	Bond Bk.	15
TASKER			
William	will	H	94
	inventory	H	168
TAYLOR			
Faithy	gdn. bond	E	240
Henry	bond (1748)*		
	inventory	E	8
Jesse Jr.	est. acct.	G	377
	inventory	I	161
	sale acct.	I	168, 171
	est. acct.	I	173
John	will	A1 pt. 1	228
	admr. bond	A1 pt. 1	238
	inventory	A1 pt. 1	244
John	will	Sup. Ct.	56
	exor. bond	Sup. Ct.	56
Mary	gdn. bond	K	403
Robert J.	admr. bond	T	78
	will	T	308
Samuel	admr. bond	A1 pt. 2	417
	inventory	A1 pt. 2	473
Thomas	will	D	14
	inventory	D	43
Thomas	inventory	I	315
TERRETT			
Alexander	committee bond	W	149
Burdett	gdn. bond	W	150
George H.	will & codicil	U	126
	inventory	U	136
William Henry	will	B	181
	inventory	B	183
	est. acct.	B	275

Name	Document	Will Book	Page
TERRETT (continued)			
William Henry	will	O	136
	inventory	T	5
	est. acct.	T	45
THOM			
William, Rev.	will	C	175
THOMAS			
Amelia	will	U	265*
David Jr.	inventory	B	396
	admr. bond	Bond Bk.	72
George	admr. bond	Bond Bk.	11
Jacob	will	J	149
	inventory	J	180
John	inventory	K	174
Mark	admr. bond	A1 pt. 1	196
	inventory	A1 pt. 1	203
Robert	will	C	44
	inventory	C	46
Thomas	inventory	E	152
William	will	B	82
THOMPSON			
George	inventory	T	233*
Joseph	inventory	C	166
	admr. bond	Bond Bk.	115
Julia R.	gdn. bond	T	334
Nathan	will	X	173
Richard	inventory	R	372
Samuel P.	gdn. bond	T	334
Vincent	inventory	V	122
	sale acct.	V	124
William	inventory	E	119
William	will	H	64
	sale acct.	I	388
William B.	will	P	3

Name	Document	Will Book	Page
THORN			
Michael	gdn. bond	H	132
THORNTON			
George A.	gdn. bond	W	79
Howard Granville	gdn. bond	W	79
James F.	gdn. bond	W	79
Margaret	gdn. bond	W	79
THRIFT			
Absolom	inventory	C	186
	admr. bond	Bond Bk.	125
Anne	gdn. bond	L	142*
Charles	admr. bond	Bond Bk.	135
Charles	will	E	352
	exor. bond	E	355
	inventory	E	396
	est. acct.	F	269
Elizabeth	est. acct.	L	174
George	will	G	310
	exor. bond	G	313, 314
	inventory	G	387
	est. acct.	L	145*
Keron H.	gdn. bond	L	142*
TILLETT			
George	will	I	458
	inventory	K	84
	sale acct.	K	85
	est. acct.	K	86
Samuel	will	K	243
TITTLE			
Richard	admr. bond	Bond Bk.	44

TOLBERT see TALBOTT

Name	Document	Will Book	Page
TOWERS			
John	will	I	336
TOWNSEND			
James	inventory	X	10
	sale acct.	X	11*
TRACY			
James Francis	will	Q	43
	inventory	Q	66
	est. acct.	Q	197
	est. acct.	V	250
Thomas	will	Q	64
TRAMMELL			
Elizabeth	gdn. bond	J	238
Gerrard	will	E	148
	inventory	E	182
	sale acct.	E	220
	est. acct.	E	221
John	will	B	85
	inventory	B	198
John	will (1784 - Frederick Co., Md. see FDB B3:194)		
William	inventory	C	253, 254
	est. acct.	D	49
	admr. bond	Bond Bk.	152
TRAVIS			
John	admr. bond	A1 pt. 2	285
	inventory	A1 pt. 2	296, 359
TREIDELL			
Frederick	inventory	J	312
	sale acct.	J	314

Name	Document	Will Book	Page
TREN			
Henry	will	A1 pt. 2	490
	inventory	A1 pt. 2	504, 521
	est. acct.	B	20, 67
TRESLER			
Catherine	est. acct.	S	325
TRIPLETT			
Ann	inventory	V	258
	sale acct.	V	267, 275
Catherine A. S.	gdn. bond	Sup. Ct.	125
Francis	will	B	195
	inventory	B	204
George	inventory	O	327
George W.	inventory	W	311
James L.	will	U	182
	inventory	U	202
	sale acct.	V	25
	est. acct.	V	150, 336
Nancy	gdn. bond	E	120
Thomas	admr. bond	Bond Bk.	175
	inventory	D	209
	inventory	I	356
	sale acct.	I	402
	est. acct.	I	403
William	will	I	183
	inventory	I	189, 363
	est. acct.	I	352
	sale acct.	I	374
TRUGAN			
Edmund	gdn. bond	G	451
Edward	admr. bond	G	129

Name	Document	Will Book	Page
TURBERVILLE			
Cornelia Lee	gdn. bond	I	413
	list of slaves	J	6
	gdn. acct.	J	80, 241, 338
	gdn. acct.	K	143
	gdn. acct.	L	294
Charles L. C.	will	I	5
George	gdn. bond	H	55
George	div. of slaves	M	69
George Lee	gdn. bond	I	413
	list of slaves	J	6
	gdn. acct.	J	80, 241, 338
	gdn. acct.	K	143
	gdn. acct.	L	294
	trustee acct.	S	416, 424, 428
	will	V	294
Harriett	dower allotted	H	444
Richard Lee	gdn. bond	H	55
	gdn. bond	I	413
	list of slaves	J	6
	gdn. acct.	J	80, 241, 338
	gdn. acct.	K	143
	gdn. acct.	L	294
TURLEY			
Alexander	will	X	80
	inventory	X	161
Ann	will	V	290
Charles	will	N	292
	inventory	N	362
Charles	gdn. bond	P	2
Charles W.	vs. Patsy Coleman - decree	T	302
George W.	inventory	O	195
	est. acct.	P	233
	est. acct.	R	54
	est. acct.	T	124

Name	Document	Will Book	Page
TURLEY (continued)			
James	inventory	C	112
	admr. bond	Bond Bk.	107
James	will	O	71
	inventory	P	70
	sale acct.	P	75
	est. acct.	Q	145, 226
	est. acct.	U	164
James Jr.	est. acct.	Q	229
Jane	will	C	50
	inventory	C	158
	sale acct.	C	159
	est. acct.	C	161
John	will	B	126
	inventory	B	207
Julia Ann	gdn. bond	P	135
Paul	admr. bond	C	141
	will	C	221
Paul	will	D	39
Sampson	will	K	57
	inventory	K	78
	sale acct.	K	113
	est. acct.	L	154*
Susan	gdn. bond	P	82
Susan	will	X	309
(widow of Alexander)	inventory	X	337
TURNER			
Charles	est. acct.	D	175
	sale acct.	D	176
	inventory	D	191
	admr. bond	Bond Bk.	148
Fielding	admr. bond	A1 pt. 1	107
Francina	will	I	367
James	gdn. bond	K	169
Kitty	will	I	222

Name	Document	Will Book	Page
TURNER (continued)			
Peter	inventory	A1 pt. 1	112
	est. acct.	A1pt. 1	124
TYLER			
Betsy	will	N	387
Charles	inventory	D	102
	admr. bond	Bond Bk.	157b
Elizabeth	est. acct.	O	424
James	will (Alexandria Co. - see FDB V2:246)		
TYNAN			
James	will	S	401
Jean	will	V	71
URTON			
John	will	L	284
VAN DUSEN			
Robert	gdn. bond	W	11
Samuel	gdn. bond	W	11
VARNALL			
George	inventory	L	206*
VAUGHN			
Cornelius	sale of slaves	J	390
Mary	will	J	333
	sale of slaves	J	390
VERMILLION			
James T.	inventory	U	357
John H.	admr. bond	Sup. Ct.	68
William L. M.	gdn. bond	U	148

Name	Document	Will Book	Page
VERNON			
John	admr. bond	F	204
	inventory	F	260
VILEY			
John	inventory	E	151
	est. acct.	E	222
VIOLET			
Edward	will	C	152
Ewell	will	C	101
	inventory	C	129
Lucretia	will	S	93
Margaret	gdn. bond	G	20
	gdn. bond	J	93
Nessey (Agnes)	dower allotted	G	191
Thompson	inventory	L	80
	admr. acct.	L	213
Thompson W.	gdn. bond	J	97, 336
	inventory	Q	174
Whaley	admr. bond	G	1
	inventory	G	17
	est.divided	G	190
	widow's dower		
	allotted	G	191
	est. acct.	G	382
	est. acct.	J	92
William	gdn. bond	G	20
	gdn. bond	J	93
WADDIE			
Mary	gdn. bond	A1 pt. 1	143, 151
WADE			
Valinda	admr. bond		71
Zephaniah	admr. bond	A1 pt. 1	170, 224
	inventory	A1 pt. 1	172

Name	Document	Will Book	Page
WADE (continued)			
Zephaniah (cont'd)	est. acct.	A1 pt. 1	219
	inventory	A1 pt. 1	224
	est. acct.	A1 pt. 1	235
	est. acct.	A1 pt. 2	407, 543
WAGENER			
Peter	inventory	C	249, 251
	admr. bond	Bond Bk.	149
Peter	will	G	404
	inventory	H	140
	est. acct.	I	129
	sale acct.	J	378
	est. acct.	J	398
Peter	inventory	O	190
Sinah	will	J	266, 268
	est. acct.	J	400
WAIGLEY			
George	will	T	201
	inventory	T	281
	sale acct.	T	284
	est. acct.	U	9
Richard	gdn. bond	T	333
WALKER			
Charles	gdn. bond	U	324
	gdn. bond	V	92
	gdn. acct.	W	268
John	gdn. bond	U	324
	gdn. bond	V	92
	gdn. acct.	W	270
Samuel	will	U	275*
	inventory	U	365
	sale acct.	U	367
	slave inventory	V	93
Samuel's children	see individual names		
	(Charles, John, and Thomas H.)		

Name	Document	Will Book	Page
WALKER (continued)			
Thomas H.	gdn. bond	U	324
	gdn. bond	V	95
WALLACE			
Samuel	admr. bond	G	123
WALLER			
Elizabeth	est. acct.	U	159
WALSH			
John	admr. bond	G	180
WALTERS			
James	sale acct.	U	47
	est. acct.	V	232
John N.	committee bond	V	94
	committee acct.	W	262
	committee acct.	X	56*

WALTERS, William see WATERS, William

WARD			
Anna	will*		
	(1851 - Prince William. Co.)		
Anna Maria	will*		
	(1853 - Prince William. Co.)		
John	inventory	C	253
	est. acct.	D	96
	admr. bond	Bond Bk.	154
John	will	I	219
William	will	F	335
	exor. bond	F	337
	est. acct.	G	395
Zachariah	will*		
	(1822 - Prince William Co.)		

Name	Document	Will Book	Page
WARDEN			
James	will	E	136
Robert	will	A1 pt. 1	34
	exor. bond	A1 pt. 1	35
	inventory	A1 pt. 1	42
	est. acct.	A1 pt. 1	140, 170, 302
WARRING (or WARREN)			
John	inventory	B	221
	admr. bond	Bond Bk.	33
WASHINGTON			
Ann E.	gdn. bond	P	131
Bushrod, Judge	will	P	350
	inventory	Q	1
	est. acct.	Q	256
	sale acct.	Q	312
	div. of slaves	Q	317
	est. acct.	R	43
	est. acct.	S	518, 521
	est. acct.	T	186
Bushrod C.	gdn. bond	I	417
	gdn. acct.	J	405
Corbin	will	H	180
Corbin's heirs	see individual names		
	(Bushrod C., Jane Mildred, John Augustine, Mary, Richard Henry Lee)		
Edward	will	F	160
Edward	will	K	106
	inventory	L	224, 246, 265
	sale acct.	L	227, 248*
	est. acct.	L	236*, 251, 266
	est. acct.	M	6, 16, 25, 34

Name	Document	Will Book	Page

WASHINGTON (continued)

Edward (cont'd)	est. acct.	N	399, 402, 409, 420
	est. acct.	P	96, 99, 110
	receipt	S	44
Edward's children	see individual names (Edward Sanford, Elizabeth Catharine, George William, John, Joseph Hough, Margaret Sanford, Mary Ann)		
Edward Sanford	settlement	M	31, 40
	settlement	N	406
	receipt	S	44
Elizabeth	will	K	1
Elizabeth Catharine	gdn. bond	L	406
	settlement	M	31, 40
	settlement	N	409
	receipt	S	44
George, Gen'l.	will	H	1
	schedule	H	15
	est. acct.	J	317, 370, 373
	inventory	J	326*
	sale acct.	J	359
	est. acct.	M	77, 80
	est. acct.	Q	262
George Augustine	will	F	243
	exor. bond	F	248
	est. acct.	H	201, 235
	admr. bond	H	202
George William	gdn. bond	L	406
	settlement	M	31, 40
	settlement	N	416
	receipt	S	44
Hannah	will	I	34*
	inventory	J	19

Name	Document	Will Book	Page
WASHINGTON (continued)			
Jane Mildred	gdn. bond	I	417
	gdn. acct.	J	405
	will	U	200
John	settlement	M	31, 40
	settlement	N	402
	receipt	S	44
John Augustine	gdn. bond	I	417
	gdn. acct.	J	405
	gdn. bond	L	285
John T.	inventory	J	255
	est. acct.	J	256
Joseph Hough	settlement	M	31, 40
	settlement	N	420
	receipt	S	44
Lawrence	will	A1 pt. 2	539
	est. acct.	B	113
	est. acct.	C	14, 16
Lawrence	will	H	52
	inventory	H	66
Lund	will	G	213
Margaret Sanford	gdn. bond	K	377
	settlement	M	31-40
	receipt	S	44
Martha	will	I	133
	inventory (1802)*		
	est. settlement (bound manuscript		
	Arlington courthouse)		
Mary	gdn. bond	I	417
	gdn. acct.	J	405
Mary Ann	settlement	M	31, 40
	settlement	N	406
	receipt	S	44
Richard Henry Lee	gdn. bond	I	417
	gdn. acct.	J	405
	inventory	Sup. Ct.	43

Name	Document	Will Book	Page
WATERS			
Sarah	will	U	341
	inventory	V	27
	sale acct.	V	48
	est. acct.	V	169, 224, 353
William	will	O	398
	inventory	P	145
WATKINS			
David	inventory	N	180
	est. acct.	O	236
	est. acct.	Q	147
David	gdn. bond	S	272
Deyo	inventory	W	294
	est. acct.	X	418
James M.	inventory	X	336
	est. acct.	X	341
Jane Ann	gdn. bond	R	371
John H.	inventory	X	336
(Not deceased; shared property with James Watkins, deceased)			
Margaret	gdn. bond	R	370
	gdn. bond	S	51, 272
	gdn. acct.	S	505
Thomas	inventory	M	167
	est. acct.	M	285
William Thomas	gdn. bond	R	370
	gdn. bond	S	51
	gdn. acct.	S	506
	gdn. acct.	U	77
WATSON			
John	inventory	C	84
WATTS			
John	will	J	154

Name	Document	Will Book	Page
WAUGH			
Alexander	admr. bond	Sup. Ct.	130
James	inventory	N	176, 308
	sale acct.	N	177
	est. acct.	N	178
	est. acct.	O	355
WEAKLIN			
John	admr. bond	Bond Bk.	84
WEBSTER			
William L.	est. acct.	M	293
WEEKS			
Sarah	will	S	452
WEIR			
Bladen	inventory	W	350
	sale acct.	X	8
WELDON			
Lloyd	est. acct.	O	280
WELLCOM			
Eliza	admr. bond	A1 pt. 2	350
WELLS			
Ibri	inventory	M	1
John	inventory	I	332, 430
Nathaniel	will	Q	418

WEST

Ann Margaret   see WEST, Nancy
(daughter of Roger)

Name	Document	Will Book	Page
WEST (continued)			
Ann Virginia	gdn. bond	M	47
(dau. of James C.)	gdn. acct.	M	230, 245
George	will	E	134
	inventory	E	326
George William	will	G	234
Hugh	admr. bond	A1 pt. 2	390
	will	B	74*
	inventory	B	77, 80
Hugh	will	C	7
	inventory	C	10
	sale acct.	D	231
	admr. bond	F	45
James	gdn. bond	I	29
(son of Roger)			
James C.	inventory	K	278
	est. acct.	L	390
James W.	gdn. bond	M	47, 245
(son of James C.)	gdn. acct.	M	230
John	will (1716)	LRLS	166
John	will	D	25
	inventory	D	50
John	gdn. bond	I	29
(son of Roger)			
John	will	I	540
	div. of slaves	J	239
	est. acct.	L	37
John Jr.	will	D	4
	inventory	D	123
	est. acct.	D	164, 170, 225
Margaret	gdn. bond	F	178
Margaret	will	G	329
Mary	gdn. bond	M	47
(dau. James C.)	gdn. acct.	M	230
Mary	gdn. bond	I	29
(dau. of Roger)			

Name	Document	Will Book	Page
WEST (continued)			
Mary Ann P.	gdn. bond	J	54, 222
(dau. of John)	gdn. acct.	N	159
Matilda Ann B.	gdn. bond	J	54, 222
(dau. of John)	gdn. acct.	N	154
Nancy	gdn. bond	I	29
(dau. of Roger)			
Roger	gdn. bond	D	219
Roger	gdn. bond	I	29
(son of Roger)	gdn. bond	K	34
Roger	will	H	217
	codicil	H	220
	inventory	I	47
	est. acct.	J	165
Sarah	gdn. bond	J	1
(dau. of John)			
Sybil	will	E	235
Sybil	gdn. bond	F	178
Thomas	inventory	C	184
	admr. bond	Bond Bk.	116
Thomas	will	I	499
William	will	F	300*
WHALEY			
Alexander	inventory	U	327*
	sale acct.	U	328
George	will	U	124*
	inventory	U	258*
	sale acct.	U	261*
	est. acct.	U	405
Gilson	est. acct.	N	94
Julia	gdn. bond	N	4
WHEELER			
Ignatius	will	I	441
Mary Ann	gdn. bond	P	6
(dau. of William)	gdn. acct.	R	24

Name	Document	Will Book	Page
WHEELER (continued)			
Rachel	will	I	302
Rebecca	inventory	B	355
	will	B	356
	est. acct.	B	397
Richard	will	A1 pt. 2	436
William Lewis	gdn. bond	P	6
(son of William)			
WHITE			
Lewis	inventory	J	105
	est. acct.	J	106
Philip	est. acct.	P	176
William	inventory	S	220
	sale acct.	S	222
	est. acct.	T	362
WHITELY			
Robert	admr. bond	A1 pt. 1	50
	inventory	A1 pt. 1	75
	est. acct.	A1 pt. 1	125, 134
WHITING			
Anthony	will	F	249
	admr. bond	F	314
	est. acct.	G	286
	sale acct.	G	287
Carlyle Fairfax	will	Q	177
Ellen Marr	gdn. bond	S	68
WICKLIFF			
Benjamin	admr. bond	Bond Bk.	85
Robert	will	D	265
	inventory	D	366
WIGGINTON			
Roger	will	B	2
	inventory	B	6, 24
	est. acct.	B	25

Name	Document	Will Book	Page
WIGGTINTON (continued)			
Russell K.	inventory	T	286
	sale acct.	T	288
	est. acct.	U	551, 231
Spencer	est. acct.	O	38
	inventory	O	62
	sale acct.	O	63
Willie E.	gdn. bond	T	82
	gdn. acct.	U	56, 231, 232
WIGHAM			
Thomas	will	J	107
WILCOXEN see **WILLCOXON**			
WILEY			
George	est. acct.	L	26
James	will	J	377
	inventory	O	72
	est. acct.	O	316
John	inventory	E	151
	est. acct.	E	222
WILKEY			
John	inventory	B	148
	admr. bond	Bond Bk.	37
WILKINS			
John	inventory	A1 pt. 2	535
	est. acct.	A1 pt. 2	535
WILKINSON			
Catherine	gdn. bond	L	374
George B.	gdn. bond	N	240
	gdn. acct.	S	232
Juliet L.	gdn. bond	p	83
Louisa	gdn. bond	L	416

Name	Document	Will Book	Page
WILKINSON (continued)			
Thomas	inventory	A1 pt. 2	492
Thomas	admr. bond	E	401
	inventory	E	409
	est. acct.	F	89
Thomas	gdn. bond	F	291
WILLCOXON			
Fanny B.	gdn. acct.	X	410
John	gdn. bond	W	21
Lewis	admr. bond	A1 pt. 1	36
	inventory	A1 pt. 1	39, 84
William	gdn. bond	W	21
William D.'s			
children	see individual names (John, William)		
WILLIAMS			
Aler	will	I	362*
	inventory	I	368
	est. acct.	L	5
	est. acct.	P	114
Burr	gdn. bond	M	258
Charles	will	V	360
	inventory	V	385
	sale acct.	V	387
	est. acct.	W	259, 261
Fielder	gdn. bond	J	161
George	will	G	29
	exor. bond	G	31
	inventory	G	87
	est. acct.	G	269
	exor. bond	G	298
George	will	N	40
	inventory	N	241
	sale acct.	N	243
	est. acct.	P	47

Name	Document	Will Book	Page
WILLIAMS (continued)			
George	will	U	261*
	inventory	X	167
	sale acct.	X	169
	est. acct.	X	377
Howell	admr. bond	A1 pt. 1	12
	inventory	A1 pt. 1	21
	est. acct.	A1 pt. 1	86
John	will	C	255
	inventory	C	255
John	will	G	299
	exor. bond	G	301
	inventory	G	336
John	gdn. bond	K	421
(son of Joshua)	gdn. bond	O	363
	gdn. acct.	P	66
John Henry	gdn. bond	U	148
Joshua	est. acct.	L	329
Josiah	admr. bond	G	16
	inventory	J	63
Kitty	gdn. bond	J	161
Lee	will	N	86
Massey	gdn. bond	J	162
	gdn. acct.	K	188
Milly	gdn. bond	K	421
(dau. of Joshua)	gdn. bond	O	363
	gdn. acct.	P	66
Nancy	gdn. bond	K	421
(dau. of Joshua)	gdn. bond	O	363
	gdn. acct.	P	66
Owen	will	C	240
	inventory	C	252
Polly	gdn. bond	K	421
(dau. of Joshua)	gdn. bond	O	364
	gdn. acct.	P	66
Rachel	division	X	266
Richard	admr. bond	A1 pt. 1	263

Name	Document	Will Book	Page
WILLIAMS (continued)			
Richard	will	X	148
	sale acct.	X	304, 400
	inventory	X	306, 388
	est. acct.	X	441
Sarah	will	G	386
	inventory	G	415
	sale acct.	G	417
	est. acct.	H	86
Thomas	will	A1 pt. 1	15
	exor. bond	A1 pt. 1	17
	inventory	A1 pt. 1	22
	est. acct.	A1 pt. 1	122
	est. acct.	B	15
Thomas	inventory	J	194
	est. acct.	N	298
Thomas	will	R	75
	inventory	R	319
William	gdn. bond	J	162
	gdn. acct.	K	188
William	admr. bond	A1 pt. 1	119
	inventory	A1 pt. 1	126
	est. acct.	A1 pt. 1	161
William	admr. bond	A1 pt. 2	272
	inventory	A1 pt. 2	282
William	admr. bond	A1 pt. 2	423
	inventory	A1 pt. 2	506
	est. acct.	A1 pt. 2	508
	est. acct.	B	88
William W.	inventory	K	290
	sale acct.	K	292
WILLIAMSON			
Henry	will	B	142
	inventory	B	179
Jesse	inventory	H	203
	est. acct.	I	338

Name	Document	Will Book	Page

WILLIAMSON (continued)

John	inventory	D	243
	admr. bond	Bond Bk.	177
John	inventory	I	400
William	inventory	E	217
	est. acct.	E	231, 317

WILLIS

Thomas	will	A1 pt. 1	214
	inventory	A1 pt. 1	232
	est. acct.	A1 pt. 2	274

WILSON

David	sale acct.	N	375
John W.	gdn. bond	N	343
Thomas	inventory	M	198
	sale acct.	M	201
	est. acct.	M	203
Thomas J.	gdn. bond	N	343

WINDSOR

Almira	gdn. bond	W	179
	inventory	W	222
Catherine	see WINDSOR, Emily Catherine		
(dau. of Newman C.)			
Elizabeth	gdn. bond	Q	84
(dau. of Newman C.)	gdn. acct.	S	295
Emily Catherine	gdn. bond	Q	84
(dau. of Newman C.)	gdn. acct.	S	296
Fanny	gdn. bond	W	179
	inventory	W	222
George	gdn. bond	E	199
	gdn. acct.	E	380
	committee bond	K	48
Joseph R.	gdn. bond	Q	84
(son of Newman C.)	gdn. acct.	S	297

Name	Document	Will Book	Page

WINDSOR (continued)

Richard S.	inventory	W	199
	est. acct.	W	346
	est. acct.	X	126r128
Richard S. Jr.	gdn. bond	Q	83
(son of Newman C.)			
Robert N.	gdn. bond	Q	84
(son of Newman C.)	gdn. acct.	S	296
Sarah	will	I	422
	inventory	K	27
	est. acct.	M	137
	est. acct.	O	282
Thomas	will	F	188
	exor. bond	F	191
	inventory	F	274
	est. acct.	F	292
	sale acct.	M	86
	est. acct.	M	139
	est.acct*	O	282
William	inventory	A1 pt. 2	501

WINGATE

Henry	admr. bond	F	257

WISHEART

Charlotte	gdn.accts	D	233
Henry	will	C	242
	inventory	D	57
	sale acct.	D	59
	bonds due estate	D	61
	est. acct.	D	62

WITHERS

Andrew F.	gdn. bond	T	219*
Elizabeth S.	gdn. bond	T	219*
H. C.'s children	see individual names		
	(Andrew F., Elizabeth S., Susannah)		
Susannah	gdn. bond	T	219*

Name	Document	Will Book	Page
WOLFE			
Catherine	gdn. bond	T	102
WOOD			
John	inventory	T	74
John	inventory	E	66
WOODWARD			
James	will	E	244

WOODWARD see also WOODYARD

WOODYARD			
Jeremiah	inventory	L	96*
	sale acct.	L	97
John Thomas	gdn. bond	T	174
Thomas	will	N	211
	est. acct.	S	198

WOODYARD see also WOODWARD

WOOSTER see WORSTER

WORSTER			
John	will	Q	50
	inventory	Q	301
	sale acct.	Q	304
John	inventory	W	209
	est. acct.	X	433
Sarah	dower allotted	Q	311

WREN			
Allen	sale acct.	L	79
	est. acct.	O	354
Gabriel A.	inventory	U	343
	sale acct.	U	345
	est. acct.	V	206

Name	Document	Will Book	Page
WREN (continued)			
James	will	K	363
James	inventory	S	275
	sale acct.	S	277
	est. acct.	S	414
James	will	U	137*
	inventory	U	139
John	inventory	L	134*
	sale acct.	L	135
John	inventory	N	106
	sale acct.	N	113
	est. acct.	O	68
John H.	will	R	410
	inventory	S	52
John Thomas	gdn. bond	U	181
Lucinda	see DAVIS, Lucinda		
Nelson	will	U	42
Richard	inventory	T	90
	sale acct.	T	92
Sarah	will	L	53*
	inventory	M	312
	sale acct.	M	314
	est. acct.	M	316
Sarah	will	U	108
	inventory	U	352
	sale acct.	U	354
Sarah H.	gdn. bond	U	181
Susannah	will	V	321
Thomas	will	C	27
	inventory	C	37

WRENN see WREN

WRIGHT			
Abraham	inventory	C	185
	admr. bond	Bond Bk.	119
		Bond Bk.	120

Name	Document	Will Book	Page
WRIGHT (continued)			
Isaac R.	inventory	W	203
	sale acct.	W	206
YANGSHAW			
Lawrence	inventory	A1 pt. 2	523
	sale acct.	A1 pt. 2	524
	est. acct.	A1 pt. 2	525
YEAMAN			
John	inventory	G	365
	sale acct.	G	368
	est. acct.	H	199
YOST			
John	will	I	357
YOUNG			
David	inventory	C	86
	division	D	352
	admr. bond	Bond Bk.	103
John	admr. bond	F	91
John	inventory	Q	92
	est. acct.	T	259
ZIMMERMAN			
Adam	gdn. bond	J	62
Catherine	gdn. bond	J	43
Henry	inventory	J	68
	sale acct.	J	71*
	est. acct.	K	46*
	est. acct.	N	284
	est. acct. (first settlement)*		
John	will	N	204
	est. acct.	W	115
John H.	inventory	X	372, 379
	sale acct.	X	381

Name	Document	Will Book	Page
ZIMMERMAN (continued)			
Kitty	will	K	344
Samuel	gdn. bond	J	62
ZUILLE			
Robert	will	D	79
	inventory	D	88